A Peachy Life

A Peachy Life

Waiting on Tables and Beating the Odds in the '60s — An Italian-American Woman's Story

Leonora "Peachy" DiPietro Dixon

CITYLIT
PRESS

Baltimore, Maryland

Library of Congress Control Number: 2011925616
ISBN 978-1-936328-04-8

CityLit Project is a 501(c)(3) Nonprofit Organization
Federal Tax ID Number: 20-0639118

Printed in the United States of America, First Edition/2p
Front Cover Image: "Peachy" Dixon in her Little Bo Peep outfit,
age 7, 1948. Photo enhanced by Robert Gussio
Editor: Robyn Barberry
Copy Editor: Donald Clark
Interior Design: Jonas Kyle-Sidell and Gregg Wilhelm
Cover Design: Gregg Wilhelm

CITYLIT
PRESS

c/o CityLit Project
120 S. Curley Street
Baltimore, MD 21224
410.274.5691
www.CityLitProject.org
info@citylitproject.org

CityLit Project's offices are located in the School of Communications Design at
the University of Baltimore. For information about UB's MFA in Creative Writing
and Publishing Arts, named one of the country's most distinctive programs by
Poets & Writers magazine, please visit www.ubalt.edu.

Nurturing the culture of literature.

I dedicate this book to my brother Vincent and his wife Grace for all of their technical help in the preparation of the book. I also dedicate the book to my sister Rosie for all of the pictures she gave me to use in the book.

I started the book just to remember all of the days of my childhood, and it blossomed into a story of my life. I would also like to thank all of my family and friends who helped me to go in the right direction with my life.

There are also two other people who helped me through all of the good times and bad times. I came out just perfect with their guidance. Thanks, Mom and Dad.

And last but not least, my brother Johnny for all of the many times he came to my rescue.

Thank you all; I love you so.

Table of Contents

Foreword

*A*ll families should have a Leonora "Peachy" Dixon in their lives. She is the keeper of stories, the historian without the fancy degrees. She is the heart overflowing with love for the immediate world. Now she has written *A Peachy Life*, and every page evokes the charm, and sometimes the pain, of life on the east side of Baltimore over the last two-thirds of a century.

How's this for a slice of long-ago Highlandtown? "My dad, Carmen, worked hard at Bethlehem Steel, at Sparrows Point. When Dad came home, he would be grimy. He needed a bath. I can remember Mom always going into the bathroom to wash his back. Dad would say, 'Phyl, come here, I need my back washed.' She would go because she always did everything for him. They loved each other very much. They were Edith and Archie Bunker in disguise. After dinner, in the summer, Dad would sit outside at the corner of the alley in a rocking chair. He used to say he was catching the breeze coming up from the alley. In his hand was a portable radio, and he would listen to the Orioles game. Before evening's end, my parents' close-knit neighbors would bring their chairs over and sit and talk to Mom and Dad until dark."

That's all. The small pleasures of the world before air conditioning and cable TV turned us all into hermits, our lives filled with so much packaged entertainment and so much self-inflicted isolation.

Peachy recalls a time of mixing together. She spent her early school years at Our Lady of Pompei and graduated from Patterson High School. Her uncle was the late city councilman Mimi DiPietro, and she worked as a waitress for John Unitas at the Golden Arm. She's been a fixture at Sabatino's in Little Italy for as long as anybody can remember. She wrote her 200-page story, she says, because, "I started this just to remember all the days of my childhood, and it blossomed into a story of my life."

But it's more than that. It's the story of all those around her, the story of lives that revolved around family and neighborhoods that were the fixtures of Baltimore and are sometimes still its greatest strength.

And it's about the sweet times we make for ourselves when we don't count on outside sources to fill our hours. How's this for a celebration? "Every New Year's Eve," Peachy writes, "Dad and Mom would have a big party at their house in the basement. Dad had dug the basement out years ago when they first moved into the house. It was six-feet deep and as long as the house, so there was plenty of room for everyone to sit around and dance. All of my aunts and uncles, on both sides of the family, would come over. My cousin played the accordion.

"Around twelve o'clock, my Uncle Fritz would get one of my mother's old bed sheets, wrap it around himself, and run up and down the street and pretend he was the New Year's Eve baby. My Aunt Lena, who was Uncle Fritz's wife, would say, 'Fritzy, what are you doing? Stop acting crazy.'

"We would all tell him to keep on going—'Don't pay attention to her; you're having a good time.' Oh, what a great time we all had, so much fun for so little money. How I miss the innocence of those times, just full of lots of laughter."

The past gets away from us too quickly. Every family should have somebody like Peachy, to write it down and hold onto the details. That way, we get to relive the glad times, and pass them on to those who weren't there, so they fully understand where they come from.

There were rough times, too. There was an abusive marriage for Peachy, but it produced two loving daughters. Money was always tight, but there were joys money couldn't buy.

There's the tale of her parent's courtship, with a parlor filled with grandparents, uncles, aunts, and priests, too, "…to make sure they weren't doing anything wrong." There's the first family car, which they proudly drove to Grandpop Gaetano's, "…who only lived right down the street from us." There's the tender scene, after Peachy's father has died, when her sister gives birth to a boy, "…and we all knew that Dad had come back to us." When a family has someone like Peachy keeping track, no one ever really goes away.

Michael Olesker

Introduction

One day while I was talking to my sister Rosie, I started to remember my past. I began telling her how nice it was when we were young living under the protection of Mom and Dad, and having Mom's tender touch and soft words of encouragement. I was lost in my childhood for a while, remembering how protective Dad was for all of us. The more we talked, the more I remembered. I could not believe how all of these memories poured out of my head. It was unreal. I wanted to tell my sister how important it is to stay connected to our family.

This book is a story of my immigrant grandparents coming to America, the virtually unknown, building a life for their family here, and withstanding all the obstacles they had to overcome just to raise their children.

My grandparents were devout Catholics and they instilled a deep faith in their children, who in turn carried their devotion on to their children—my brothers, my sister, and me. My grandmother was always helping out at church. She was the person who initiated the union between my mother and father. Mom was the secretary for Our Lady of Pompei Church. When Dad saw Mom, he fell instantly in love with her, but Mom's father strongly resisted the union between my parents. However, through the persistence of Dad's mother and with the help of the priest from the church, love prevailed.

It's the love story of Mom and Dad. My father could not get enough of Mom. He loved her so much, and Mom in turn did everything for him. All of Mom's brothers and sisters adored their wives and husbands. They were truly committed to each other, so unlike in today's world, when you hear about so many divorces. Their love was a lasting love; the kind that revealed itself when they looked into each other's eyes.

When my paternal grandmother was alive, I could understand everything that she said to me because I could also speak Italian.

When I asked her to teach me Italian, she would always say, "English, English, speak English." She wanted me to talk to her in English. Grandmom said that when she came to America people embarrassed her and called her a dumb "dago."

It is a story of a young girl, me, growing up in a warm, loving Italian family, with all the affection that you could not believe possible in one person's lifetime. During the years of growing up, there were many family parties for special occasions or just a simple gathering for an excuse to eat some delicious homemade food. In the hurry up world of today, when families live all over the country, it was so different to have all my relatives living in close proximity. Everyone was there to help out in times of crisis and everyone was there in times of joy. We were all Italian and the most important thing in our lives was family and food, all homemade and all delicious.

It is a story of the closeness we had with neighbors and how we all respected one another. We became friends in this small neighborhood called Highlandtown, which was located in east Baltimore, Maryland. When Dad bought the first TV on the block, all the neighbors and some of our family members would congregate in the living room watching this new invention. Highlandtown was a popular place to live because in addition to good people, we had all the conveniences like the butcher, the baker, the chicken store with fresh eggs, the bank, the post office, the library, the novelty store, the department store, and so on. How lovely it was to be surrounded by all these marvelous people, places, and things.

After attending nine years of Catholic school, I entered public school. This experience was one of the most dramatic ones in my life. After being under the strict direction of nuns, I was suddenly allowed to make my own decisions about what courses I wanted to take.

I also had two wonderful brothers. They were so intelligent that they were able to attend college to further their education. One brother majored in science and physics long before it was the popular thing to do. The other brother focused on the financial world. Both of them acquired great jobs. Most importantly to me, they were always there to help me along the way.

But life's path wasn't always so easy. After growing up in such a caring family, my life turned into a world of both physical and mental abuse from a husband that put me through a horrendous marriage. The only good thing that came out of the marriage was my two lovely children. I took many beatings from this man, even if I just answered him the wrong way. After the beatings, he would leave me alone to heal my wounds. I had no idea why he was treating me this way or when this violence would stop. I just kept thinking he would change, but he never did.

I was learning about drugs in the '60s, something I knew nothing about. They took over my husband's life and turned him into a drug-crazed person. The addiction was so bad that drugs consumed his life, but I had two little children who depended on me. I had to save them from this monster and the horrible life he made for us.

All of which inspired me to record the events of one life hoping they would in turn help other lives. I wrote this book to inspire women to stand up for themselves and to encourage women to know that they do not have to take abuse from anyone. I want to help women to understand that with the help from God, your family, and friends, you can make it. Have confidence in yourselves. Take the initiative to stand up for yourselves. You can do it. I know if I walked away from seven years of this awful abusive marriage, you can too. I want this book to aid women who are suffering in abusive marriages to come out of their shells and take charge of their lives. I believe that if you stand tall and put your mind to it you can not only survive, but thrive. You can accomplish whatever you want to make of yourself. I want to stress to you the importance of a close connection with your families because they will always come through for you when they see that you are sincere.

I had to devise a plan to leave my husband who did not care about me or our children. I had to make a decision fast to come up with a way to support my children. I met a person who changed my life for the better and encouraged me to become a waitress. She gave me the confidence to move on with my life and make changes. She told me that waitressing was easy and I could do it. She told me that after becoming a waitress I would have money to provide shelter, get medicine, and buy food for the children. When I finally made the move, I felt so relieved. The burden was lifted.

Venturing into a world of the unknown, I went head first into the job of waitressing. After many blunders, I landed a job at a restaurant owned by my heroes, Johnny Unitas and Bobby Boyd. During this time I met many famous people and to my surprise they treated me as their equal. The excitement of waiting on football stars and movie stars set my head whirling. Just to be in their presence and having the opportunity to serve them amazed me.

While I worked at the Golden arm, I met new friends, went to the Super Bowl in Florida, and really started coming into my own as a woman. But times were not so friendly for women. I tried to buy a car, but could not get a loan because the dealership told me I needed a man's signature on the note. I was flabbergasted! I was the one who paid all the bills, but the system was against women.

I then went to work at a German restaurant called Haussner's, which looked more like a restaurant that had popped up in a museum. Pictures lined every inch of wall and statues surrounded every table. Their food and desserts were so incredibly good that people lined up around the building every evening.

Then I came to work at Sabatino's, one of the busiest Italian restaurants in Baltimore's Little Italy. Everything was homemade and made to order. At this restaurant I met so many wonderful customers, movie stars, politicians, entertainers, musicians, artists, and athletes. Most of the customers came to the restaurant repeatedly and, because I saw them so often, I developed a close relationship with my regulars.

I hope this book provides some perspective of how wonderful family life was back in the 1950s and '60s. I also want to describe how difficult it was to take care of my children in a world when women had to prove themselves in everything that they did, but how one woman had a "peachy life."

Tutto il mio amore!

Peachy

One: Out of the Cradle

I grew up during a simpler time in a quiet little place called Highlandtown in east Baltimore. People walked the streets at any time of the day or night and never worried that anything would happen. We slept with our doors and windows open at night without worrying that someone would break into the house. Everyone was friendly and neighborly and we all tried to help each other out. We all knew other people's circumstances, their ups and downs, their hardships and joys.

Everyone's immediate family lived in the same neighborhood. For me, this included my aunts, uncles, cousins, and grandparents. If you lived in Highlandtown in the mid-twentieth century, you knew someone in your family would always be close by to help you out in case of an emergency.

I was born on Friday the 13th, and if that was not enough of a bad omen, my baptism was held the following month on December 7, 1941, the same day the Japanese bombed Pearl Harbor. With these two strikes against me, you might guess that my life would be full of turmoil, but in my close-knit neighborhood, everything and everybody appeared safe to me.

3510 Claremont Street

Our house was a rowhome located near the corner of an alley on a small city street called Claremont Street right off of Conkling Street, which was three blocks from Eastern Avenue, Highlandtown's main shopping district. My home was a wonderful place. As soon as you walked in the door wonderful smells coming from Mom's kitchen greeted you. And then Mom would flash her beautiful smile and would ask, "Do you want something to eat or drink?" Everyone felt welcome right away.

In the living room with a large window there was a big sofa, two end tables, lamps, and a recliner that was Dad's, with an ottoman for him to rest his feet, and on one side of the recliner was a small telephone table.

Dad made a wedged recliner to prop himself up and watch TV while lying on the floor. He made this object out of wood that he bought from the local lumber company. He wrapped foam and fabric around the recliner that he purchased from our neighborhood supply store, at the corner of Conkling and Claremont Streets. The store was called Conkling Salvage Exchange foam shop. Mr. Mike, the owner, was a very accommodating person who always helped his customers. He especially took care of his neighbors. He sold everything for all occasions—Christmas, Easter, summer, winter. Mr. Mike also sold artificial flowers and wreaths for placing on graves, along with material and foam for making cushions for things like the wedged recliner that Dad made, which he invented way before anyone else.

The living room spilled into the dining room, which was another large room with a window. It had a dining room table and chairs and another couch that opened into a bed, mainly used when members of the family spent the night. The next room was Mom's kitchen with a large table and chairs, china closet, stove, refrigerator, sink, and another large window. Dad made the kitchen larger than a normal kitchen so that Mom had plenty of room to move around and cook her wonderful dinners for all of us.

In the back of the kitchen, Dad had extended the house and added a bathroom, which included a bathtub with fancy legs, a toilet, and a window. The back door led out into our beautiful rose garden. Dad built the addition when my parents first got married because they lived on the first floor and their kitchen was then in the basement. They rented the upstairs to help cover their expenses. After I was born, my parents took over the whole house because they needed room for their growing family.

My bedroom was in the back of the house. I had inherited my Grandmother Gelsomina's feather bed, which consisted of two long pillows, stuffed with soft, fluffy feathers. The room was cold in the winter and hot in the summer. My two brothers slept in the middle room on twin beds. They had no privacy at all, and there was just one window. It was a huge room with no closets that opened toward the stairs and the hall that led to the bathroom. The bathroom door did not completely close from all the layers of paint Mom put on it every year.

Mom and Dad's room was in the front of the house. Their room was large with a high ceiling and two large closets. It had two large windows and two doors. One door was always closed for privacy while the other door was left open. When my sister Rosie was born, they put the crib in their room.

The house also had a basement that Dad dug out practically by himself. He made it six-feet high and as long as the house, about sixty feet. Because Dad was short, he considered six feet a high ceiling. He white washed the walls so that the basement would always be clean, and it was especially immaculate because of Mom and Dad's impeccable cleaning habits.

The backyard rose garden blossomed with twelve beautiful rose bushes that Dad planted in 1938. Every year he fertilized the garden and took such special care of it, so that even today some of the rose bushes still thrive. Our garden also included two fig trees that produced so many pieces of the soft, light-bulb-shaped fruit that Italian's consider a delight. We broke the figs open and let the juices run into our mouths. Italians wait anxiously every summer for the trees to yield the sweet juices from this wonderful fruit that tastes absolutely delicious.

Mom

Phyllis DiPietro had chubby cheeks and brown eyes. She was beautiful, with a little nose and soft features. She wore her thin hair just below her earlobes. Mom never dressed fancy, normally wearing a floral printed housedress with her slip showing just ever so slightly. She was an extremely modest and shy person who loved to take care of her children and her husband, Carmen. She was a little on the heavy side, although she always tried to watch her weight because she had diabetes.

Her father, who was a little stocky, died from diabetes. When he got a sore on his foot, the doctors wanted my grandmother to have his leg amputated. Grandmom adamantly refused, so the doctors called my Aunt Jenny, Mom's sister, into the hospital to try to persuade Grandmom to let them amputate Grandpop's leg. Aunt Jenny would not agree to this procedure either because she did not want to go against her mother's wishes. Sadly, a little while after this episode Grandpop became dreadfully ill and passed away. Therefore, Mom really tried to take care of herself so nothing like what happened to Grandpop would happen to her. Who would take care of us if she became sick?

Mom kept the house spotless all the time. My aunts always commented, "You could eat off of your kitchen floor, it is so clean in here Phil." Mom was always cooking one of her delicious dishes, such as her homemade chicken noodle soup or her fabulous tomato sauce or her homemade chili con carne. These dishes took her hours to prepare, so the smells went all through our home, and all the people who walked by the house knew she was cooking one of her special dishes. She worked diligently over the stove cooking her delicacies for hours at a time or she stood at the sink doing dishes. Mom was forever doing everything for each and every one of us.

Dad

Carmen DiPietro worked extremely hard on the swing shift at Bethlehem Steel, one of the largest shipbuilding companies in the world, located seven miles east of Highlandtown in Sparrows Point. His job at the steel mill consisted of binding steel coils after they were produced in the coke ovens. The men at the steel mill mixed the coke with iron ore to produce the steel. The coke ovens burned so hot that they belched red dust that settled on everything. The awful stuff covered all of the homes and cars in the area like rusty snow. When Dad came home from work, he was grimy with red dust.

The work was hard and dirty, but Dad always had a big smile on his face when he came home. When he smiled, his high cheekbones pushed his cheeks into his bright sparkling eyes. He had an oval face with a large nose. His round stomach expanded from eating all of the wonderful food that Mom cooked for him. When he flexed his huge arms, his muscles looked exactly like the cartoon character Popeye's.

But he used those arms gently to hug his children.

The Courtship of Mom and Dad

Before Mom and Dad were married, Mom worked in the office at Our Lady of Pompei Church doing clerical work for the priests. Previously, Mom and her sister Mary worked at Johns Hopkins Hospital serving food to the nurses, who were fed sit-down meals. Mom and Aunt Mary arrived at the hospital by 5 a.m. to perform their chores. Because of this early arrival time, they were allowed to stay at a house across the street from the hospital. While working there, they were subject to the hospital's strict policies, although they considered themselves lucky to have a job. They earned just $4.50 per week and were paid once every two weeks, bringing home only $9 every two weeks to give to their parents. Still, this little bit of money helped the family pay some bills. Then, when the war broke out, there were more jobs available for everyone, so Mom took a position at Our Lady of Pompei.

Meanwhile, Dad's mother was an active parishoner who was always doing something special for the church. Grandmom Annarella spent as much time as possible at church to get away from the situation at her home, where she was in a very unhappy marriage. Being at church surrounded by other people from Italy comforted her. When she first saw Phyllis, she could not wait to tell Carmen that he had to come to church and meet a beautiful lady who worked there.

Social gatherings took place at the church hall on most weekends. These affairs helped the neighbors to have a little fun apart from their very busy weekdays. Everyone brought food and all of them had a great time eating and dancing. At these affairs, the priest always asked Mom to sing because she had a beautiful "operatic" voice. While she was singing, Dad saw her and her beauty overwhelmed him.

Dad wanted to ask Mom out, but this was difficult for him because Mom's father was very strict. So Dad devised a plan with his mother and several of his siblings to go to Phyllis' house and try to win the approval of her parents. The priests also went over to talk to my grandparents. They assured them that Carmen came from a good family and that he was honest and hardworking. The priests and Grandmom Annarella left when finished talking to my mother's parents, leaving Carmen, Phyllis, and Dad's two sisters in the parlor listening to music on the Victrola. My grandfather sat in the middle of the parlor with his cane watching all of them to make sure they were not doing anything wrong. Because my grandfather was from a learned family, he was unsure about his daughter getting involved with a working class person. Grandmother Gelsomina whispered to him from the kitchen, "Pssst, pssst, come here." Nevertheless, my grandfather pretended not to hear her and sat there watching their every move.

The next day, Dad called Mom at work to ask her if everything was okay. She started crying and said, "Oh, Carmen, my father thinks you are rowdy and won't let me go out with you."

Dad was determined, so he and the priests thought of a plan that would allow him to see Mom. The priests told my grandparents that they were taking Phyllis to the movies with them, and then they would pick up Carmen, too, and they all went to the movies together. The priests had so much confidence in Dad. They knew he would not do anything to hurt Mom, and this is how their courtship began.

The Wedding

My grandmother Annarella was the main person who helped Mom and Dad get together. She knew Mom was a wonderful person because she was at church every day and saw all of her good traits. Because of Grandmom's persistence, Mom and Dad were allowed to date, and soon after they won the approval of my mother's father wedding plans began. Mom's dress was beautiful and she looked absolutely gorgeous in it. Her sister, Jenny, who was as bashful and shy as Mom, stood for Mom as the maid of honor, and Dad's cousin Fred, who was a happy-go-lucky guy, was best man.

My parents married on September 26, 1937, at Our Lady of Pompei Church by Father Scialdone, who was the pastor at the time. All of Dad's family and Mom's family and all of their friends and neighbors attended their beautiful wedding. They rented a hall right down the street from the church where a band played and everyone danced for hours into the evening. With a huge cake and plenty of food, it turned out to be one of the best weddings ever, mainly because of the love that my parents had for each other. When they looked into each other's eyes, they shared a lasting look of love seen by everyone present at their wedding and every time they were together. In those days men looked for someone to spend their lives with and build a family, someone to live with forever.

After the wedding Dad took Mom to 3510 Claremont Street, the house in which they would reside for the rest of their lives. The house was near the church, Grandmom and Grandpop DiPietro's house, and not too far from Grandmother and Grandfather DelGiudice's home either. They wanted to surround themselves with their families every day.

Mom and Dad's Simple Lifestyle

Mom served dinner every evening at five o'clock sharp when Dad arrived home from the steel mill. He came home covered in red dust and grime, so immediately took a bath. He called out, "Phil, come here, I need my back washed," and into the bathroom Mom went because she did everything for him.

They loved each other so much. Dad always quoted some "proverbs." Mom always tended to everything for him and us. She was the reason Dad worked so hard to keep his family fed and clothed. We never wanted for anything, and I never understood how Dad and Mom managed to accomplish so much with so little. Mom would always fix my hair in beautiful long curls. She would always take time out of her busy day to make her children look simply marvelous. With the little that Mom had to work with, she accomplished amazing feats.

After dinner, which we ate together every night, the children went out and played with friends while Mom and Dad talked to their neighbors. In the summer, Dad sat outside on the corner of the alley in his chair. He said he was catching the breeze coming up from the alley. He listened to the Orioles game on the portable radio he held in his hand. Before evening's end, my parents' two closest neighbors always brought their chairs over and sat talking with Mom and Dad until dark.

Mom's friend Irene was short and beautiful with short black hair. She looked just like a movie star. When Ms. Irene walked down the street, all the men turned to look at her gorgeous figure. Her husband, Mr. Matthew, was short like Dad with thin brown hair. He worked hard with Dad at Beth Steel. Ms. Irene and Mr. Matthew had two children. Their son Matty was short and cute with brown hair and glasses. He played with my brother Johnny. Their daughter Elaine was a pretty little thing with huge curls in her hair that her mother fixed for her every day. Ms. Irene dressed her children well and was just as tidy as my mom. Her daughter Elaine and my sister Rosie played together, and they became close friends.

Lucy was a friend of mine who lived across the street. She and I played jacks for hours at a time. Lucy had brown hair and brown eyes and was short and thin. She smiled constantly and laughed a lot, mainly because she beat me at jacks all the time. Life was simple then because we amused ourselves with simple things.

Some summer nights would be so hot that Dad would bring all the mattresses downstairs and we would all sleep on the floor. We kept the doors and windows open and never worried that someone would break in. One morning, when Dad could not stand the heat anymore, he went to our favorite store, Epstein's on Eastern Avenue, and came home with a huge fan. We wheeled the thing around from room to room because the fan was the only thing that would cool us off.

My parents frequented many stores on Eastern Avenue. One was Silver's Shoe Store located at 3724 Eastern Avenue right near our favorite place—The Popcorn Store! Silver's Shoe Store provided good shoes at discounted prices. Mr. Max Silver took care of his regular customers by finding us bargains because he knew that most of his customers had large families. If he took good care of them, they would buy shoes at his store for a long time.

The Popcorn Store was a small place, but they had a huge popcorn machine that popped the corn right in the store-front window. When people saw all of the popcorn jumping about right in front of them, they could not resist buying some. They also sold caramel popcorn that smelled irresistible and melted in your mouth. Often when Mom finished shopping, she stopped at the store to buy some of these delicious morsels for us.

Shopping centers did not exist at this time. Everyone shopped on "The Avenue" because anything anyone ever needed for themselves or their home was available at stores along Eastern Avenue. All the store owners on "The Avenue" ate lunch at Pozanek's Restaurant because they cooked their corned beef themselves and served kosher food because so many of the merchants were Jewish. At dinnertime, Pozanek's served regular food like steaks, crab cakes, and hamburgers. On Saturdays, when the wives of shop owners would go shopping, the men gathered at Pozanek's for drinks while waiting. Later in the evening, the wives met their husbands at the restaurant for dinner. It was a familiar meeting place where everyone enjoyed good, reasonably priced food.

Phyllis DiPietro,
Peachy's mother,
1935.

Phyllis and Carmen,
wedding photo,
September, 26, 1937.

Peachy, Johnny, and
Vince DiPietro on the
stoop in front of their
Highlandtown home at
3510 Claremont Street,
Baltimore, Maryland,
1948.

Two: Coming to America

*M*y grandmother Gelsomina DelGuidice, my mother's mother, was a caring and loving individual. Mom looked exactly like her. She had very soft features that accented her beautiful face. Later in her life, she wore thick glasses because her eyes grew weak from all of the sewing she did to help make ends meet. Many times Mom told me how hard my grandmother had it when she first came to America.

They arrived from Italy in 1914. My grandmother Gelsomina's family owned an extraordinary vineyard on top of a hill in Naples in the region of Atripalda in southern Italy. The vineyard overlooked the Tyrrhenian Sea's beautiful clear water, which twinkled like a thousand diamonds. People from all over Italy journeyed to my grandmother's home to buy grapes for winemaking. My grandmother told Mom that when she was in Italy her family was rich because they had such a great business selling grapes; however, they made the decision to go to America—the land of plenty. But not long after they arrived the Great Depression hit and it was not easy to find good paying jobs.

Grandfather DelGuidice's Job

My grandfather Raphael was tall with a sharp nose on which his glasses rested. He dressed impeccably every day with a white shirt, suit, and tie, so everyone thought he was rich. Even though my grandfather was a lawyer in Italy, he could not practice law here in America because he could not acquire a license. He had the gift of gab, and neighbors flocked to Grandfather's home for advice because he was so intelligent and knew the law. Neighbors called him Reguidice, which meant that he was a "king," because he helped them with their problems.

He got a job working for The Metropolitan Life Insurance Company selling insurance. He rode the streetcar for long hours and collected money that people owed him for their life insurance policies. He went from house to house collecting money from his clients. Sometimes it would only be a dollar or a few cents, but back in the 1930s, a dollar was a lot of money. He told my grandmother that some of the people thought he was using the money for his own purposes. It was only when one of his clients died, and Grandfather brought the family their insurance money, that people started to believe and trust him. Grandfather worked hard because he wanted his children to have a good education, but college was impossible to afford during The Depression and all of his earnings paid for the family's expenses.

With all the Italian immigrants flooding New York City, the Metropolitan Life Insurance Company assigned my grandfather to New York because he spoke Italian. Raphael thought it would be a better opportunity to provide for his family, so they packed up and the insurance company moved them. While Grandfather was in New York, he became the orator in the Sons of Italy where he was highly respected. One time there was a sick child near death who needed to be baptized immediately, so my grandfather was asked to stand for the child during the baptism. The parents, who were also Italian, lived in New Jersey and belonged to the Sons of Italy, which is why he was asked to stand for their child. Guess what the child's name was? Francis Sinatra! Many years have passed, and I have no way of verifying this, but Mom told me this story and so did my uncle Joe, and they both insisted it was true. All of the people who were involved have passed away, so I will never find out if it was really the famous Francis Albert Sinatra.

While in New York, they lived in an apartment that was like a "commune." They shared a bathroom with all of the other people who lived on their floor. The bathroom was all the way down the hall, and they had to wait their turn with everyone else to use it. The apartment was not a clean place, but my grandmother worked hard to keep it immaculate because she was a very tidy person.

While they lived there, a huge horse died and was left in the street for such a long time that it decomposed and was covered with maggots. The smell was unbearable and they had to walk past this horrible sight every day to get to their apartment. My grandmother could not wait until they went back to Baltimore. She was pregnant with Uncle Romelo and she wanted to go home to have the baby.

My grandparents had rented their house to their neighbor's relatives. But when they came back to Baltimore, the tenants did not want to move out of the house. The renters also did not make payments on the house, so my grandparents almost lost their home. They had to leave their furniture in the moving van for two days under a bridge and move in with friends while they waited for the tenants to move out. My grandfather straightened out matters with the building and loan company. It was a good thing that he was a well-educated person; he could talk his way out of anything because he had the gift of gab. He did not want to lose the house because they had lived there for such a long time.

After they came back to Baltimore, Grandmother Gelsomina got a job sewing buttonholes on coats to help pay expenses. In the meantime, Grandfather's diabetes got progressively worse. The doctors at Johns Hopkins Hopsital, where he went for his treatments, wanted to amputate his leg, but my grandmother would not have it. As the disease progressed, it took its toll on his body and finally took his life in 1940. After he died, my grandmother worked long, hard hours sewing buttonholes to make ends meet. The work ruined her eyesight and she was left wearing extremely thick glasses.

In the meantime, the war began in Europe, and everyone worried about family back in Italy. The beautiful village of Naples where my grandparents grew up was destroyed and rendered families poor. Grandmother Gelsomina worked hard to send her family clothes and other items to help out, even though my grandmother was living in poverty herself. Times were hard for everyone then, and all of the children pitched in by getting jobs to help pay the bills.

The Birth of Brother Johnny

When Mom went into the hospital to deliver my brother, Johnny, Vince and I were sent over to Grandmother DelGiudice's house to stay with her. I was only two years old then. Needless to say, being of Italian descent and being the grandmother she was, she tried to fatten Vince and me up. We had such a great time there with her; she was always doing something for us. One day while we were playing in the basement of Grandmother's house, she actually found us in the middle of the coal bin. We were black from head to toe, but Grandmother did not scold us. She just took us upstairs, gave us baths, and fed us some more. Every time we did something she rewarded us with food, the true Italian way, so when we came back home, we had both gained weight.

At home we found our little brother Johnny waiting for us. He had a round face and his hair was light brown and a little roly-poly body. Mom would forever take good care of all of us, but somehow Johnny was always closest to her.

Sometime after this, a great sadness came over Mom. My grandmother Gelsomina, who was such a pious woman, went to Mass every morning to pray for my uncles. They had joined the Navy to help my grandparents with their money situation, but Grandmother was extremely worried for their safety. So she went to church every day to pray for their well-being and their safe return home. She must have prayed extremely hard because my two uncles both arrived home unharmed. Only their hearts were broken because Gelsomina died before they could get home.

The winter of 1944 into '45 was bad with a lot of snow and ice everywhere. Early on the morning of January 30, Grandmother Gelsomina left the house for Mass like always. Since the sidewalks were icy, Grandmother stepped out into the street where she was hit by a car and killed. If the driver had stopped to help her, she might have lived. The accident happened under a bridge, so maybe the driver did not see her since it was still dark that morning and she was dressed in black, which she wore everyday since my grandfather passed away. We do not know how long she laid there before someone came to help her, but by the time Mom and the rest of her family found out about it, Grandmother had died. Everyone knew what a hard life my grandmother had; it just did not seem right for her to be killed this way.

Police caught the driver of the car, but nothing happened to him because back then a hit-and-run was not considered a serious offense. The case went to court, but the man was not charged with anything and was dismissed. All of my aunts and uncles were upset by the way she had died, and that the man did not get any kind of punishment. All of her children were distraught and they missed her terribly. Mom practically stopped eating; she became so thin after her mother's passing.

Mother's Siblings

Mom had two sisters and two brothers, and they were all close. Aunt Jenny was the one who kept in contact with Mom every day. Jenny was shy, short, and thin with curly hair and grey eyes. She was also exceptionally religious because my grandmother raised all of her children as strict Catholics. Aunt Jenny displayed religious pictures all around her home, where every other Sunday we visited her and Uncle Ernest. They had three children—Charles, Ezio, and Ernie. Uncle Ernest was tall and thin with a heavy Italian accent. He had blonde curly hair, which he passed on to his three boys. He was a chef by trade, but he knew that the only way his three boys would get ahead was through a good education, and he saw to it that they all went to good schools. Their huge house off Belair Road had a large backyard where we children played while the adults chatted during these Sunday picnics.

Mom's other sister was Aunt Mary, who was also religious because of her strict upbringing. She had long black hair, and was a little taller than Mom with warm, smiling eyes. Her great government job allowed her to take time off to travel. She was the daredevil type; nothing seemed to bother her. She came and went as she pleased because she never married and did not have any children. She hoped to visit all the holy places in the world, and during one trip to the Holy Land severe fighting broke out in Israel. Mom was so afraid that something would happen to her, but such things never fazed Aunt Mary. Aunt Mary lived in an apartment downtown close to the Basilica of the Assumption, the first roman Catholic Cathedral in America. "Holy grounds" she considered it. She kept Mom and me informed about all the events happening in the city. Aunt Mary was another strong person who constantly involved herself in my life and looked out for my well-being.

Mom had two brothers: Uncle Joe (his Italian name was Sabina) and Uncle Romelo, the baby of the family. Uncle Joe joined the Navy because there were no jobs and he needed to help his parents pay bills. After Uncle Joe was discharged from the Navy, his friend Guy took him to meet a gracious woman named Dorothy. When the war started on December 7, 1941, Uncle Joe was set to be drafted into the Army, but he rejoined the Navy. After Uncle Joe met Dorothy, he knew that he wanted to spend more time with her. This was the beginning of their long courtship. Aunt Dorothy and Uncle Joe loved each other and wrote to each other the whole time he was stationed in England. Uncle Joe could hardly wait to come home and be with the love of his life. They had that special love because when they looked into each other eyes you just knew they were truly in love. They planned their beautiful wedding, and Uncle Romelo was supposed to be the best man, but he could not come home in time. So Aunt Dorothy's brother, Anthony Palmerino, stood as their best man and her sister, Marie Palmerino, was the maid of honor. They got married on July 1, 1945, and had a long and happy life together. He rose every morning at 4:30 and ran for an hour, come home, made coffee, and took it to Aunt Dorothy to wake her up. They were the picture of a happy couple.

Uncle Romelo was Mom's baby brother. He was tall and thin with lots of thick curly brown hair and smiling eyes that would light up the whole room. When he laughed, everyone laughed with him. His brother and all of his sisters would watch out for him. Mom was the oldest child, and she was the one who had to take care of him. My grandparents were busy trying to provide for their family. Mom told us that one time she took Uncle Romelo to watch the fireworks on the 4th of July in Patterson Park. It was not far from her home, and by the time they were ready to leave Patterson Park it was dark. She walked around the park with her little brother for three hours, and she could not find her way home. When Mom found a phone booth and called her parents to tell them what happened, they told her to ask a police officer to help her find her way home. The police officers acted as though Mom was putting them out for asking them for help, but eventually they took her home.

When Uncle Romelo grew up, he was absolutely handsome. He joined the Navy because jobs were scarce and he had to help his parents with expenses. He was stationed on the ship called the *U.S.S. Saturn*. It was a supply ship that brought supplies to boats stationed in the middle of the ocean. One time while the ship was docked in Bayonne, New Jersey, all the sailors went to an Italian restaurant called the Key Hole in Union City. The place belonged to a man named Guy De Martino. In the restaurant was a large bar, and at the end of the bar was this beautiful, short, dark haired young lady named Mary, who worked there as a cashier for her uncle. When Uncle Romelo entered the restaurant, he noticed Mary right away because of her outstanding good looks. One of Mary's girl friends, Kitty, who also worked there, told Mary that the cute sailor wanted to meet her. Mary's friend arranged for the meeting, and this is how their courtship began. They waited until Uncle Romelo got out of the service before they got married on September 9, 1947, at Our Lady of Grace Catholic Church in Fairview, New Jersey.

Uncle Joe DelGiudice, his brother, was the best man, and Aunt Mary's sister, Rita D'Anna, was the maid of honor. Mom, Aunt Jenny, and Aunt Dorothy all went up to New Jersey for the wedding. Dad could not go to the wedding because he had to work. When my aunt and uncle first got married, they came down to Baltimore almost every weekend to visit with Uncle Romelo's family. He wanted to stay close to his family forever.

The Tonsil Operations

Dr. De Marco was a special friend of my DelGiudice grandparents. He looked exactly like my grandfather, and as a member of the Sons of Italy, he did not charge my parents a high fee. Mom took us there all the time when we were sick, and sometimes he would make house calls. One time he told Mom that Vince and I had to have our tonsils removed because we were forever getting colds. The doctor told Mom if he took our tonsils out, it would eliminate all of our sickness. Dr. De Marco performed the tonsillectomies on Vince and me right on the kitchen table. He came into the house with his assistants carrying ether and medicines. I only remember how bright the kitchen looked. Mom covered everything with clean white sheets. The French doors leading to the dining room and the door to the bathroom were closed. Pots of water boiled on the stove in case Dr. De Marco needed sterile water.

One at a time, we went on top of the kitchen table to have our tonsils removed. Though I was very small, the thing I remember most was how white and bright the room was with all the sheets and the huge lights that Dr. De Marco brought. I am certain Dr. De Marco performed the surgery as a favor to my parents since they did not have a lot of money.

When we look back on that day, Vince and I think it was almost a miracle that we survived and that the house did not blow up. There were flames under the boiling pots of water and there was ether—there might as well have been a bomb in our house! Plus we could have gotten some kind of a serious infection. A Highlandtown kitchen is not as sanitary as an operating room no matter how many white sheets and bright lights and pots of boiling water there are.

Nevertheless, here we are, alive and well today.

Left: Gelsomina and Raphael DelGuidice with Joe and Phyllis, 1917.
Center: Vincent and Peachy, 1942. Right: Vince and Peachy after Holy
Communion in front of Claremont Street home, May 1945.

Jenny Borchini and Phyllis DiPietro
at Joe and Dorothy DelGuidice's
home in Woodlawn after Gelsomina
DelGuidice died, April 1945.

Three: Famiglia DiPietro

My Grandparents DiPietro were married in 1901 in Italy and came to America in 1905. They lived in a village to the east of Rome called Coroppoli Teramo in the Abruzzi Province of Italy. My grandfather Gaetano was in love with Grandmom Annarella's sister and wanted to marry her, but according to Italian custom, the oldest daughter had to get married first. So Grandpop married my grandmother, but their marriage was not a happy one. They were civil to one another, but there was no love between them. They never looked into each other's eyes like my mother and father did.

Grandpop worked very hard farming, but the job did not pay much. He was poor and had a wife and three children to support. People kept telling Grandpop how great it was in America. Grandpop's sister, Adelaide, and his brother, Fiorinde, were already living in America, and they finally persuaded Grandpop to come to America.

When my grandfather decided to leave Italy, my grandmother realized she was not going to see her family again. This was very upsetting to her, especially as a young mother. One of their sons, Pasquale, was young and wanted to stay in Italy with his friends; in fact, while they were boarding the ship Pasquale ran away. Grandmom was hysterical, but Grandpop said that they had to go on to America because everything was arranged.

The trip to America was not pleasant for her. Grandmom was pregnant with Dad; Carmen was going to be his name, and with all of these issues on her mind, she did not have a great experience on the boat. Her first-born son had just ran off and was still in Italy, while everyone else was on their way to America. Grandmom already had two other children, Dominic and Mary, and was pregnant with her fourth child, so she had her hands full on the boat. Dominic was very little then, and a nice Italian boy named Bernardino Di Pasquale helped to take care of Dominic for Grandmom because she was so ill, her stomach was upset during the whole trip to America.

Although immigrants were not allowed on the top decks, the people who worked on the ship felt so sorry for my grandmother that they let her come up on-deck so that she could have some fresh air.

When they first landed in America, Grandpop and Grandmom DiPietro resided in Dunbar, Pennsylvania. My Grandfather's brother, Fiorindo, and sister, Adelaide, lived in Baltimore, and they persuaded him to move. The family moved to Baltimore and resided at 3812 Claremont Street, where they lived for the rest of their lives.

Visiting Dad's Parents

On Sundays, we would go to visit my grandmother Annarella and grandfather Gaetano. They only lived right down the street from our home, but we would still all pile in the car and Dad would drive us down to Grandmom's house. My grandfather would be sitting outside with his cane in his hand, right on the corner as if he owned it. Everybody said he looked exactly like President Truman, with his glasses, his size, and his mannerisms. People kidded him about this as they passed him by, but he loved all the attention.

Dad and Mom both came from large families. Dad's brothers and sisters would also visit my grandmother's house on Sunday. It was a meeting place where everyone gathered to have fun; you could say we had a family reunion every Sunday. Because my father was bow-legged, his siblings gave him the nickname "Boh." That's how much fun and good humor they had with each other.

My Dad's Siblings

Aunt Lena was one of my grandparents' youngest children. She was lovely, and thin with long black hair. She was forever bringing the family together for one thing or another. She loved these gatherings with her brothers and sisters. Her husband, Uncle Fritz, was tall and extremely handsome, a stately fireman.

He was the most congenial of all the brothers-in-laws. All of us children loved him because of his fantastic personality; he was constantly making us laugh. Aunt Lena wanted all of her siblings with her at all times because she was at her best when they were all together. She got her strength from them.

Uncle Mimi lived at Grandmom's, too. Everyone called him the "Mayor of Highlandtown" because he looked out for the community's well being and all of the people who lived there. He was short and stocky and looked exactly like my Dad with a little less hair. Actually, all the brothers and sisters looked alike because they all had my grandmother's full face and large hands.

Uncle Sammy, who has epilepsy, also lived there. Because not much was known about the disease back then, Uncle Sammy was not allowed to attend school, so he was slow and child-like all of his life. Everyone would play with Uncle Sammy because he was like a big kid, and all of us kids would aggravate him so much. He had chewing gum with him at all times, and we bugged him until he would give some to us. He was also short and stocky, and he wore his pants with big suspenders to hold them up.

The adults all gathered together talking in Italian, so we children were not able to understand anything they were saying. My sister said the grownups would be talking about sex, which is why they would talk in Italian.

My cousin Clara's grandparents lived next door to my grandparents. Her grandmother, Adelaide, was my grandfather's sister. Her family would visit their grandparents on Sunday, and we all played with one another, and became friends as well as cousins. We always stayed amongst ourselves, because we knew better than to interrupt the grown ups. "Children are supposed to be seen and not heard," my father said. It was one of Dad's favorite expressions, along with "respect your elders." He repeated these two sayings to us day in and day out.

My grandmother was such a jolly person, with a smile on her face at all times. She had a round face and huge hands. She wore a black dress, and underneath the dress was a big white petticoat with a huge pocket. She would reach inside of her pocket and give her grandchildren something, but it was hush, hush so no one else would know. She had a big smile, a hug, and a shiny silver dollar for each and every one of us.

Dad's oldest brother was Uncle Pat. He was always laughing and was short and a little on the heavy side with a huge crop of hair. He was married to Aunt Annie, who was slightly taller than Uncle Pat. She was also on the heavy side with brown hair, and she wore glasses. They had three boys: Tommy, Louis, and Freddie. They would bring them to Grandmom's and Grandpop's on Sunday and we had a close relationship with the boys. Uncle Pat and Aunt Annie owned a bar located in Essex not far from Highlandtown, and we would also visit them sometimes on Sunday, because my aunt and uncle could not get away from their business.

Aunt Mary was tall and thin with short brown hair and was Dad's other sister. She was married to Uncle Alex, who was a thin, medium built man with brown hair and glasses. They had five children—David, Edward, Gloria, Julie, and Mary Rose—who also came to our grandparents' on Sundays. Aunt Mary and Uncle Alex lived around the corner from Grandmom.

Uncle Joe was Dad's other brother and was married to Aunt Tina. They had two children—Carl and Kathleen—who also came to Grandmom's and Grandpop's on Sunday. We would all play together. Uncle Joe and his family only lived down the street from us, and we would also go to the same schools together with their children.

Uncle Charlie was another brother of Dad's and he was married to Aunt Esther. They had three children: Ronald, Glenda, and Elaine. We would play with all of our cousins while we were at our grandparents' house. While the grown ups were together, we had our own get together.

Dad's Lost Paycheck

I can remember Dad telling us the story of the time he lost his pay envelope in 1926 when he was nineteen. When Dad worked at the Point, the workers were paid in cash. He left work just as he usually did and got on the streetcar to come home, and that was when he discovered he had lost his pay envelope. He was beside himself because he knew he was in a lot of trouble if he lost his pay. He got off the streetcar and backtracked everywhere he had been before looking for the envelope. By the time he gave up it was late. All of his brothers, cousins, and friends—who all worked at the Point because it was the only good-paying job in town—had gone home. He was all alone and he did not know anyone who would lend him money to take the streetcar home. Dad wound up walking all the way home from Sparrows Point to Highlandtown, which is about a ten-mile walk.

When Dad arrived home, he was met by his worried mother. Dad was a reliable person who was on time for dinner every night. Dad would tell us if you were late for dinner, you did not get fed. His parents had seven children, and it was hard feeding all of them. After he told his mother what had happened, she picked up her skirt, and gave him some money. She said, "Carmen, here is some money for you, and be quiet and don't say a thing to your father, and I won't tell him what happened to you."

My grandmother knew if he told his father, he would not believe him and he would have probably gotten a beating. In those days, they would say, "Spare the rod and spoil the child." This was another one of my Dad's favorite expressions. Grandmom was Dad's savior, and he never said "no" to her. Whenever she asked him to do anything, he was constantly there for her. Dad was really touched by the kindness she showed him. Even as a grown man, he went to her home to repair whatever was broken. He was always one of her favorites.

Grandfather DiPietro's Job

Grandfather DiPietro owned a bakery in Highlandtown. The bakery was right in the basement of the house. They delivered bread to the neighbors by horse and carriage for two cents a loaf. He sold bread to the whole neighborhood and everyone came to him to buy dough to make their own bread and pizza. He had a great business. He was partners with his brother and sister, and they made enough money from the business to bring the rest of their family over from Italy. Then, they all worked together at the bakery. Both of the brothers and their sister developed pneumonia and were hospitalized. They lost a lot of their business and it was hard to retrieve the customers that they lost. Then my grandfather's brother Fiorindo decided to move to Essex and left the business to my grandfather and his sister, Adelaide. Grandfather then sold the business and went to work for the railroad, making $8 a week.

Years later, while waitressing at Sabatino's in Little Italy, I met a man who owned a bakery located in Highlandtown near my grandparents' house. When Mr. Tsakalos found out who my grandfather was, he told me that my grandfather sold him his business. Grandpop Gaetano even took him around and introduced him to all his customers. So my grandfather helped Harry Tsakalos start his business with his father-in-law Steve Paterakis—the famous H&S Bakery.

Left: Gaetano and Annarella DiPietro at 3812 Claremont Street, April 1951. Grandmom DiPietro at Our Lady of Pompei Church Hall near intersection of Claremont and S. Conkling streets in Highlandtown, May 1955.

Back (l-r): Joe DiPietro, Lena Jansen, Sammy DiPietro, Mary DiSalvatore, Mimi DiPietro. Front (l-r): Carmen DiPietro, Charles DiPietro, Pat DiPietro.

Four: Italian Style

Every New Year's Eve, Dad and Mom had a huge party in the basement of the Claremont Street house. Dad dug out the basement years ago when they first moved in, so at six-feet high and as long as the house there was plenty of room to sit around, dance, and have fun. Mom took care of the food and Dad bought a keg of beer. All of the Aunts and Uncles on both sides of the family would come over. Cousin Carl played the accordion and we all had a wonderful time dancing, laughing, and eating.

My cousin Carl was good looking, tall and thin, with brown hair. He was the son of Dad's brother Joe and Aunt Tina. Carl's parents were an attractive couple who loved to dance and had won many dance contests. Uncle Joe looked just like Dad, although he was a little shorter. He had lost several fingers while working at Bethlehem Steel. Many accidents happened there, but they were mostly kept from the public. His wife, Aunt Tina, was tall and elegant, with short red hair. She had a beauty shop down the street from our home where everyone from the family and neighborhood went to get their hair done.

Around midnight, my uncle Fritz would get one of Mom's old bed sheets, wrap it around himself, and run up and down the street pretending to be the New Year's baby. He would yell, "Happy New Year, Happy New Year!"

His wife, Aunt Lena, would say, "Fritzy, what are you doing? Stop acting crazy, and get inside."

By then he had a few beers in him, and he was feeling just fine. Everyone else told him to keep on going, "Don't pay attention to her; you're having a good time." We all had a good time, and for very little money.

I loved the gatherings with my huge, enthusiastic family. These innocent times were filled with lots of laughter and no worries.

Another Uncle

Sometimes on Sunday, if we did not go to Grandmom's, we would go visit Dad's other brother, Uncle Pat, who was always in a good mood. He had the same round face and large hands as my grandmother and he looked exactly like her, always smiling. He had a full head of hair, not like his other brothers, and all of his children looked like him. Mom and his wife, Aunt Annie, became friends. They both had diabetes, so they had something in common to talk about. When my aunt and uncle came over to our house for a visit, Aunt Annie would take all of her pills at the same time.

"I don't think you should take all of those pills together, Annie," my mother said.

"Oh don't worry Phil," Aunt Annie replied, "I think they all know where they are supposed to go."

Aunt Annie and Uncle Pat had a bar with the best jukebox ever. When we visited them, I would stand in front of the jukebox and dance. My cousin, Freddie—who was close to my age, and my favorite—always made me laugh. The oldest son, Tommy, was in the service. He met a girl named Joan and they fell in love. The family didn't seem to like Joan much. I could not understand why they treated her like an outsider when she was such a nice person. Later on in life, I found out why—it was the "blood." She not Italian and they didn't respect her. It was always all about the "blood."

When we got older, we would poke fun at these prejudices. When we met at family functions, we all laughed about the times when Aunt Lena lined us up to take a picture. She would say, "Only the blood." It became a joke with all of us, so before she had a chance to say it, we would all chime in, "Only the blood for pictures over here, and the non-blood for pictures over there." We can laugh about it now because we know how she is and that she won't change.

Sister Rosie's Birth

I remember when my sister Rosie was born. She was very delicate. Mom was in the basement washing clothes when she said to me, "Oh my goodness, we have to call someone! I have to go to the hospital."

I believe her water broke, but I was too young to understand what was happening to her. Uncle Joe, Dad's brother, was the only one home at the time. He took Mom to the hospital to have the baby, and what a beautiful baby she was. My parents adored her. A popular song at the time had the lyrics "O, Rose Marie, I love you, and I'm always thinking of you," so every day when Dad came home, he sang this song to my sister.

Dad wanted to get a record player so that he could play the song to my sister. He went to the TV store that was right up the street on Highland Avenue. The store was owned by a family friend, Mr. John, who was tall and thin with a warm smile, a mustache, and glasses. When Mr. John showed Dad the TV and record player combination, flashing his big smile, Dad fell in love with it. He bought it instantly, and within days, it was delivered to our home. Dad didn't buy it for himself though; it was for Rose Marie. He was always doing every-thing for his children. He just had to have the record player so he could play the song for my sister when he came home from work.

It seemed to Mom that after Rosie was born Dad was rejuvenated. He went on a shopping spree. After he bought the TV, he bought a new car—a 1950 Chevy from Charlie Irish Chevrolet on Eastern Avenue. Mom was getting nervous because he was spending money on all these luxury items. She was worried that he was going through a stage in his life where he wanted to purchase things that he had been deprived of most of his life, but she knew there was not that much money to go around. Fortunately, the car was Dad's last big purchase, and it lasted him for a long time because he took excellent care of it.

Our First TV

When Dad bought the first black-and-white TV on our block, it was more like a piece of furniture than an entertainment device. In the evenings people filled our house to gaze at the new thing, so we would sit there in front of the TV watching roller derby. Those wom-en got so rough with each other. They pushed, shoved, and knocked each other down; it was like women wrestling on roller skates. Sometimes we would sit there and watch the test pattern, which was just the number of the TV station, Channel 2. Even though it was really nothing, we thought we were watching something special. It didn't matter to us because we could not get our fill of this new invention.

Dad was an avid Orioles fan. We would have to sit in front of the TV set and watch the ballgame with him. We could not go anywhere until the Oriole game was over. After being in all week long, Mom wanted to get out of the house and go out for a ride on Sundays for a little while, but we had to wait for the Oriole game to be over. Dad used to play baseball when he was young, and because he loved the game so much, he wanted us to love it also. So there we all sat in front of the TV watching the Baltimore Orioles play ball. This is the reason why I love the Orioles today. His enthusiasm for the game has rubbed off on my children and me.

Our weekly meals always followed the same pattern. As a practicing Catholic family, we were not allowed to eat meat on Friday. Mom fixed a dish on Fridays called Pasta e Fagioli that consisted of beans and spinach. It was supposed to have pasta in it, but for some reason Mom never put pasta in the soup. It could have been because we had pasta on Sunday, and of course, it was left over on Monday. We had to eat it on Monday because you could not waste any food. Then we had it on Thursday because Dad could not wait until Sunday to have his pasta. But we could not eat pasta on Friday because the sauce had meat in it; therefore, we had it left over on Saturday. Then we had pasta again on Sunday, because this was the traditional Italian Sunday meal.

However, there was a problem with the Pasta e Fagioli. Vince did not like spinach and I did not like beans, so we swapped these pieces of food back and forth. I do not know how Dad never saw us doing this because he sat at the head of the table. I am sure he knew what we were doing, but he just did not say anything as long as we ate all of the food on our plates. We had to belong to the clean plate club, which meant you had to eat everything on your plate. Dad did not want us to waste anything.

The topic of conversation at every dinner was always the same. Dad would always be talking about how he wanted to buy a graveyard plot for him and Mom to be buried in. The other topic of conversation was about our bodily functions, such as going to the bathroom. It became so bad, I would say, "Dad, can we please talk about something other than going to the bathroom and buying graveyard plots while we are eating? I don't want to talk about you dying."

He would reply, "These are two really important things to talk about. If you don't go to the bathroom you will become sick, and if you become sick then you might die, and so I want to know that I have a place to be buried before I go."

I did not want to hear of this and I would beg him to stop.

(As it turned out, Vince, Johnny, and I had to buy the graveyard plot after Dad died. It was positively horrible. We were so upset about losing our father, but we still had to go out and buy his graveyard plot.)

I often wonder what happened to all of those people who ate meat on Friday. Today, Catholics are allowed to eat meat on Friday, but when I was a little girl it was forbidden. Did those people who ate meat on Friday back then when they weren't supposed to really go to hell? Did God forgive them, or what?

Recipe for Pasta e Fagioli (spinach and bean soup):
2 large onions, peeled and sliced thin
6 stalks of celery
(mainly the leafy ones diced, they have more flavor)
2 cans of chicken broth
2 2lb. bags lima beans
2 boxes chopped spinach or ½ box elbow macaroni
1 ½ tbsp. salt
1 ½ tbsp. oregano
10 pcs. basil, diced
2 tbsp. parsley
½ tsp. dry hots

In a 10 qt. pot, place all the ingredients except for the spinach or macaroni, and fill the pot to the handles with cold water. Then cook for 2 hours. Then add the spinach or the macaroni, and cook for another hour. Serves 6.

The Happy Days

Mom would make a wonderful dinner every evening for the whole family that included a huge salad served along with a fresh loaf of Italian bread. Mom told me all the time that the secret to making food taste good was always in the mixing. Our salad consisted of only lettuce, tomatoes, and onions to which she would add olive oil, vinegar, salt, and pepper and then mix the salad thoroughly until it tasted just superb.

Dad would make a huge production out of sharpening the knives to cut the bread. He would place two knives together and sharpen them, until they were perfect. It would only take one slice to cut all the way through the bread. Up until this day, I thought it was the man's place to sharpen knives because of the big production Dad made out of it. But, of course, he made everything seem special, as did Mom. Dad would sit at the dinner table in his tee shirt with his huge muscles showing.

Saturdays were a highlight for us. Every Saturday morning either Dad or Vince would cook breakfast for the family. They would make large quantities of never-ending pancakes and huge amounts of bacon. What a treat for all of us to be gathered around the kitchen table for this wonderful feast. Eating together was our favorite pastime; we would laugh and talk about what we were going to do for the weekend. While we ate, Mom and Dad told us stories about when they were growing up and how their family life was. It was always about family—"La Famiglia." They told us that staying together would make us strong and that we should watch out for one another.

Later in the day, Mom and I would perform all of the weekly chores during which she listened to the radio. She sang along with the opera singers with such a mesmerizing voice. We always teased her and said that Dad married her because he thought she was going to be a big opera singer.

My parents named me Leonora after the heroine from a famous opera, *Il trovatore*. Mom told me the opera was about a woman who broke several men's hearts. Of course this was not the case for me in my life. Every time I ever fell for someone, he would break my heart. Mom said there was an argument over my name. Dad wanted to call me Adrian. Guess who won?

On Saturday, we cleaned the whole upstairs, changing the sheets and towels and making everything fresh and clean. Mom loved to keep the house spotless. Mom kept everything in its place, and therefore, even though we had very little money, the house looked fantastic. After cleaning the upstairs, Mom and I would go out front to wash the marble steps. I cleaned the steps with her special soap while she washed the front window and cleaned the pavement as well as the street in front of our home. Mom wanted the front to be clean for Sunday when all the neighbors walked by on their way to church. The constant cleaning roughened her hands. By the end of cleaning day her hands were wrinkly from being in water for long periods of time. I believe this is the reason why my sister and I are such clean freaks. We had a great teacher.

Meanwhile, Vince helped Dad in the garage repairing whatever needed to be fixed from the house. Dad showed Vince how to repair things so they would not break again. Then they washed the car or took care of some jobs. Those two would spend the whole weekend together.

Our Neighborhood Baker

A fantastic baker named Mr. Thomas lived down the alley from our house. On Saturday evenings, marvelous smells wafted up toward our home. Mr. Thomas made the best donuts ever. His chocolate-covered donuts and honey-dip buns were delicious, and his marshmallow donuts were over-stuffed. We went to the bakery early Sunday morning to buy these marvelous treats so we could have our special morsels when we came home from Church. Everything Mr. Thomas made was just fabulous. Our neighborhood was full of many specialty stores, so we really did not have to go far from our home to purchase anything that we desired.

Christmas Time

Every Christmas our house would be filled with great things. Vince was born on December 15th. Therefore, Dad had to do something special for him. He went out and bought a Lionel train set, which Vince has to this day, still in its original boxes. Dad built an elaborate platform to hold the train that was absolutely gorgeous. There were mountains and train tracks, little houses with a light in every one of them, a park with children playing, and of course the beautiful manger, also lit up. The big production would begin each year on Vince's birthday and stay up throughout the holidays.

Eventually, Dad would buy a fresh Christmas tree, and we would all help decorate it. Dad and Mom would constantly involve us in everything. It would always be a big family affair.

When we got older and I visited Mom and Dad's for Christmas, I would always bring presents for everyone. I loved my parents so much, and I just wanted to show my appreciation for everything that they did for my children and me. While I would be bringing presents into the house, Dad would say "Lunga vita Roosevelt," which meant "Long live Roosevelt," because the President had created jobs for everyone. He would repeat "Lunga vita Roosevelt" over and over again.

Mom would prepare all of the different cookies for the Holiday Season—pizelles, biscottis, and cookies of all different shapes and sizes, all homemade by her.

The recipe for Mom's pizelle cookies:
6 large eggs
1 ¾ cup of sugar
1 cup butter
½ bottle vanilla extract
½ bottle anise extract
3 ½ cups all purpose flour
1 teaspoon baking powder
Spray oil on the iron as needed
Powdered sugar to sprinkle on pizelles.
Beat eggs at medium speed. Add sugar, beating until thick. Add butter, vanilla, and anise. Mix well. Add flour and baking soda. Beat until smooth. Spray pizzelle iron, and heat for 2 minutes. Place 1 teaspoon of dough on each cookie plate, and close iron. Cook for 30-40 seconds until desired color. Sprinkle cookies with

powdered sugar before the cookies are cooled off. Makes about 3 ½ dozen cookies.

Every Christmas Aunt Mary and Uncle Romelo would visit us from New Jersey. They had two small children, and my brothers, sister, and I would play with them. Because Uncle Rome and Aunt Mary came from such a distance, Mom wanted to make everything perfect for their family. She would make her homemade pasta and homemade gnocchi, and meatballs.

Here is the recipe for Mom's gnocchi:
5 lbs. large russet potatoes
2 large eggs
4 cups of flour worked in
Cook potatoes with skin on. Peel potatoes once cooked and mash on counter through a ricer. Once the potatoes do not have any lumps and are cold to the touch, mix in 2 eggs well. Then add the flour to the mixture, only 1 cup at a time. After you get the dough to the perfect texture (very moist not thick) then cut the dough into large balls. Then take one ball at a time and roll it until it is about 1 in. thick. After this, you cut the dough into little shapes, using flour to roll the dough. They should be about 1 to ½ inch each. You can make an indention with a fork or your finger if you like or leave just like this. Once all the shapes are finished, place the gnocchi in boiling water until they surface, and then cook them for 3 minutes. Place gnocchi into the sauce right away after you strain them so they will not stick together. Serves 6.

Before you make the gnocchi, you have to prepare the sauce, which took Mom around three hours to cook.

Mom's tomato sauce recipe:
4 tbsp. extra virgin olive oil
1 lge. Onion, peeled and diced
4 tsp. crushed garlic
3 large cans tomato puree
2 tbsp. parsley

1 ½ tbsp. oregano
12 tbsp. chicken broth
1 lb of beef cubes
Sauté the onion in the olive oil along with the beef cubes; then add the garlic and sauté them together. Add the tomato puree cans and all of the other ingredients bring to a boil and then let it simmer for 3 hours stirring it occasionally. Serves 6.

Here is the recipe for her homemade pasta:
3 extra large eggs
3-4 cups all purpose flour
2-4 tbs. water
Beat the eggs well in a large bowl. Add 1 cup of flour and dash of salt, and beat this until it is well blended. Work in the remaining flour and water. Knead the dough gently, and divide the dough in half. Pass the dough through a smooth roller of the pasta machine's widest setting, all the while sprinkling a generous portion of flour on the dough. Repeat rolling the dough until it is pliable. Continue moving the dough through the roller until the desired thinness is reached. There is another piece of the pasta machine that makes the dough into thin stripes like spaghetti. After you place the dough through the thin strip of the machine, place the dough on the table and flour them. Place the noodles in a 3 qt. pot of water, and add 1 teaspoon salt and 1 tablespoon olive oil. Then cook the noodles for 2 to 3 minutes or until they are tender. Serves 6.

While Mom prepared all her wonderful food, she would have a job for every one of us. We had to line up the gnocchi and the homemade pasta on the table so that they would not stick together. We were always all together, one big happy family, just the way my parents wanted us to be. Those days bring back so many good memories. As much as I try to get my little family together for the holidays, it never seems the same since my parents are no longer with us.

Mom would also make her special brasciole for Uncle Rome and Aunt Mary.

Here is the recipe for Mom's brasciole:

Brasciole is best when you make it with flank steak.

You have to pound the meat down, so it will be tender after you cook it.

2 lbs. flank steak

8 pcs. Provolone cheese

2 tsp. crushed garlic sprinkle inside a little

Add a little parsley, oregano, basil, dry hots, and salt

Roll the steaks up and tie with cord. Sautee the Brasciole in olive oil until brown on both sides, then place in sauce and cook for three hours. Serves 2 to 3.

Top: DiPietro family at New Year's Eve party, 1949. Mimi, Esther, Charlie, Carmen, Sammy, Tina, Joe, Lena, Alex. Front row includes Vincent, Johnny, Phyllis, Glenda, Pat, Grandpop DiPietro, Mary.

Middle: Johnny, Vince, Rosie, and Peachy eating pasta e fagioli at the dinner table, July 1950.

Bottom: Christmas, 1968. Carmen DiPietro with Michelle, Anna, and Johnny at 3510 Claremont Street.

Five: Good Times with the Family

*A*unt Dorothy was a tall, thin, and gracious lady with long black hair. She had a sweet disposition and treated our family fantastically. Nothing seemed to bother her. She would tell Mom, "You worry too much, Phil." She was married to Uncle Joe, Mom's brother, who was the most comical person in the family, constantly telling us jokes and making us laugh. He was short and balding with huge eyes as big as Al Jolson's. You could not help but smile with him.

While they were dating, Aunt Dorothy's father, Mr. Bernie, would go to the end of the car line at Edmondson Avenue and Cooks Lane and pick up Uncle Joe to bring him to their home to visit Aunt Dorothy. One February there was a terrific storm with snow so deep that Mr. Bernie could not pick up Uncle Joe. Her father told her, "He's not going to come here tonight, it's too bad out." They were in for a big surprise. It was Aunt Dorothy's birthday and Uncle Joe wanted to be with her so much that he walked several miles in the snow to her house. When he arrived, Mr. Bernie knew that Uncle Joe really loved his daughter.

Visiting Aunt Dorothy and Uncle Joe was an excursion because they lived all the way on the west side of town. Whenever we ventured beyond Highlandtown, Dad made us feel like we were going to the end of the earth. Before leaving, Mom and Dad made us eat a sandwich, so we would not act as if we were starving when we arrived. In fact, before we went to visit anyone, Dad made us eat something. He said, "You never know if they are going to have food or not." Of course, when you went to Aunt Dorothy and Uncle Joe's house, there would be such a great assortment of food, so we never worried about having enough to eat. It was the true Italian tradition to eat and eat and eat (*mangia, mangia, mangia*).

My aunt and uncle had three children: Bernie, Ralph, and Joey. My brothers, sister, and I had a great time playing with them, while the grownups would talk among themselves as usual.

One Christmas Aunt Dorothy gave Mom a Betty Crocker cookbook, and that was it. Mom turned into "Betty Crocker" herself. She was already a great cook, but after this, she became an excellent baker, too, and started making all of those fancy desserts.

There's No Place Like Home

After we visited Aunt Dorothy and Uncle Joe, on the way home, sometimes Dad would get lost. When we left, it was dark and there were lots of trees everywhere. Sometimes, do not ask me why, but we would be heading to Washington, D.C., instead of Baltimore. It got so bad that Uncle Joe would have to show Dad the way out of the woods. When Dad finally found his way home, he started to sing his special song, "There's no place like home, there's no place like home." He and Mom would start laughing. She was so short you could hardly see her from the back seat of the car. Actually, Dad was not tall either, but he would wear a big black rim hat, which made him look tall.

Going Out for a Sunday Drive

When Mom would get ready to go out, she would prepare herself by putting powder all over her face and then brushing some of it off. She would then put on rouge and lipstick, which then she would blot some off because she thought the lipstick was too dark on her. She was beautiful and she really did not need a lot of make-up. She was an extremely modest person. A few years ago, when my daughter Anna and I were shopping, we found a powder that smelled exactly like Mom did. We went to the store and bought one for my brothers and sister so we could all have her essence with us forever. The fragrance is called Nantucket Briar.

Our Special Summer Treats: Milkshakes

On hot Saturday evenings Dad would take all of us for a drive to the foot of Broadway where there was a wonderful ice cream store that made special milkshakes. They tasted so delicious, and as an added bonus, we got to keep the rest of the milkshake left over in the mixer. We thought we were really getting something extraordinary. This was one of our special treats from Dad on those hot summer nights.

There was a confectionery store in our neighborhood that sold the best snowballs in town. The owner, Mr. Brown, was a roly-poly man with blonde hair and a funny personality. With a joke at the ready, he would always make you laugh when you came into his store. Mr. Brown's son, Albert, was Vince's best friend. Mr. Brown's wife was a short, slender woman with black hair. Their store stayed open late in the summer to serve these fabulous snowballs, which were crushed ice topped with sweet flavored syrup. They had every flavor imaginable, plus ice cream or marshmallow on top. The simplest things made us happy then.

Summer was my favorite time of the year because there were so many activities going on. Besides our annual carnival at the end of the school year, we would also have our year-end school picnic. We would go to Gwynn Oak Park or Carlin's Park because they had the best rides in town. Mom would pack a picnic lunch for us to eat and she would even fix our table special with a tablecloth, so we would have a nice place to eat. Then she would give us the passes to go on the rides and told us to go and play. Before we left, she warned us not to hurt ourselves or do anything stupid. As we were running to get on the rides, she said, "Don't forget to come back at lunch time." Of course, once we were on the rides, we did not think of anything but having fun. There were rollercoasters and Ferris wheels, bumper cars, merry-go-rounds, and just about every ride imaginable. At evening's end, we boarded the bus to go home. What fantastic fun-filled days we had.

Italian Picnics

During the summer, Dad would take us to Bay Shore. This was a sandy beach and picnic park in Essex, which was about a half hour from our home. Mom would pack a big lunch. We piled into the car drove over a shaky bridge to get to the beach, but after we got there, we had a fabulous time. We spent the whole day swimming, sunning, and eating. Before long, the rest of our family would meet us there. Aunt Lena, who was also a great cook, would bring her delicious spaghetti and meatballs to the shore. While everyone else would be eating sandwiches, we would be having our true Italian meal.

> *Recipe for Aunt Lena's sauce:*
> *4 tbsp. Extra virgin olive oil*
> *1 lge. onion, peeled and diced*
> *4 tsp. crushed garlic*
> *16 pieces of fresh basil*
> *½ tbsp. dry hots*
> *1 ½ tbsp. Oregano*
> *2 tbsp. Parsley*
> *2 tbsp. Red wine*
> *2 tsp. sugar*
> *4 tbsp. Chicken broth*
> *6 cans crushed tomatoes*
> *Add a pound of beef cubes and a pound of pork for flavor. Sauté the onion in the olive oil; then add the garlic and sauté together. Sauté the beef cubes and pork until they are browned on all sides. Add crushed tomatoes and all of the seasoning, sugar, and wine, and simmer for two hours. Serves 6.*

The Cautiousness of Dad

One time while we were at the beach, Vincent and Johnny were playing baseball over on the other side of the picnic area when Johnny was hit in the eye with a baseball. Well that was it. We all had to pack up and go to the hospital to make sure Johnny's eye was all right.

We all sat in the hospital emergency room in the heat of the summer without air conditioning worrying that something might be seriously wrong with Johnny, but fortunately he only got a black eye and his eyesight would be just fine. I thought we would all be punished, but we were not. All we had to do was go to bed early and be thankful that Johnny was all right.

4th of July

On the 4th of July, my favorite holiday, we would always go to Aunt Esther and Uncle Charlie's home. Uncle Charlie, who was the tallest of all the brothers, was always a happy-go-lucky kind of guy, because he was with the love of his life, Aunt Esther. Uncle Charlie was the most even-tempered person on Dad's side of the family. He acted as if he did not have a care in the world, probably because of the great love that he shared with my aunt. They lived in Dundalk, which put on a huge parade every 4th of July. The floats in the parade were absolutely gorgeous! There were marching bands and majorettes a-twirling and all kinds of celebrities in the parade, which lasted for hours. Sometimes even Uncle Mimi DiPietro rode in the parade.

Later on in the evening, there would be a fantastic fireworks display. I loved the fireworks. Uncle Charlie knew just where to sit so that we would be able to get a good view of them. They would always put on a great display of fireworks that would last for a half hour to 45 minutes. Each sparkly explosion was prettier than the last.

When we went home, we would watch Dad's favorite movie, "Yankee Doodle Dandy." I loved James Cagney. He was such a great dancer. I believe I loved July 4th best because it was one holiday that had so many special events, and we had a great time through our childhood, always with the family.

St. Bernadette

I can remember the time I was in a play in grammar school. I played the part of St. Bernadette, the saint that the Blessed Mother appeared to in the town of Lourdes, France. In the vision, the Blessed Mother told the child that there was water where she was kneeling. St. Bernadette said, "Where is the water Blessed Mother? I can't find it." The Blessed Mother told her to dig with her hands in the dirt, and she would find it. She told her to wash her face with the dirt. St. Bernadette did what the Lady told her to do. St. Bernadette started to dig in the dirt, and lo and behold, up came a stream of water. The Blessed Mother told St. Bernadette the stream was full of holy water, and if people would come and wash themselves with it, they would be blessed. So, I had to wash my face with dirt on stage. Every year, thousands of pilgrims travel to Lourdes to acquire the holy water to put on their bodies to cure themselves of their sickness.

After this play, I wanted to become a nun. I often visited the motherhouse of the nuns from Pompei. The nuns would take us on day trips to visit their mother home in Trenton, New Jersey. The very peaceful home made you feel like you wanted to stay there forever. I was overwhelmed with the tranquility of the place. There were several girls in my neighborhood who also went away to become nuns, which also drove the desire in me. But when Mom found out what I was planning to do, my big idea was stopped. Mom said that I had my whole life ahead of me, and if later on I still wanted to be a nun, I could do so. She just wanted me to wait and see what the future had in store for me, but if she only knew what lay ahead, I am sure she would have let me become a nun. Although Mom's discouragement was the end of my wanting to be a nun, I was always at the nun's house. I ran errands for them, ironed their clothes, and did anything that I could to help them. In fact, my whole family was involved in the church because of my gracious grandmother Annarella.

Grandmother Annarella, who could not speak English, was constantly trying to acquire money for the church, which they greatly needed. Even though Grandmom could not speak English, she would go to the merchants (who were all Jewish) from the Eastern Avenue district and ask them for their support to help out the church. The merchants knew that most of their customers were from Our Lady of Pompei Church, and if they helped the church, they would also be helping themselves by keeping the community alive.

Top left: Carmen and Phyllis DiPietro pause in front of 3510
Claremont Street, April 1970. Top right: Peachy and her mother,
Phyllis, after May Procession at Our Lady of Pompei Church, May
1947. Bottom: Annarella DiPietro with Father Spiritti and Father
Tuturro at Our Lady of Pompei Church hall, May 1955.

Six: Catholic School Years

I had great nuns as teachers when I went to school at Our Lady of Pompei. The second grade nun, Sister Norma, is the person who gave me the part of St. Bernadette in the school play. The fourth grade nun, Sister Angelica, wanted me to be a nun like her. She is the person who asked me to come to their house to help them after school and on Saturdays and who took me on trips to the mother-house in Trenton. Later on, Sister Angelica taught my children when they went to Pompei.

I would put my alarm clock under my pillow so I would not wake any of the other family members when I got up early in the morning to go to Mass with my cousin and close friend Clara. I discovered the meaning of the Mass at this early age and found out that the Eucharist was the most sacred part of the Mass. Clara and I were little angels then, just coming into our own realism of life.

Grandmother Annarella also went to Mass every morning. I sat near her and after Mass she would give me a big hug and kiss. When we came home, Clara and I would study for our tests so the information would be fresh in our minds when we went to school later that morning.

My brothers were altar boys, and the priests would call them to serve Mass, weddings, and baptisms. Clara and I sang in the church choir. After church one Sunday we were all standing around talking amongst ourselves when Father Petti, our pastor, came over to talk to us. He pinched my cheeks, and said, "You have uh, uh…peachy cheeks." When Clara heard this, she began to laugh, and from then on, she called me "Peachy," a nickname that would stick with me throughout my whole life.

Father Petti treated all of the girls who sang in the choir well because he appreciated our volunteer work. He would take us on little trips. In the summer, he drove us down to the local shore and treated us to a day at the beach. Once a year he paid for us to go on a day trip and we always chose to go to New York City. This would be our treat for singing in the choir all year long. He paid for us to go see a Broadway show and have dinner. One time, Father Petti took us to see "The Music Man." Clara and I went backstage to see if we could get a glimpse of Robert Preston. The show was so magnificent and Mr. Preston was such an outstanding singer that we were mesmerized by him. It was our first Broadway musical, and we were so impressionable then. Father Petti was upset because he didn't know where we were. Clara and I got into a lot of trouble because Father Petti thought that we were lost somewhere in "The Big Apple." When we finally got to see Mr. Preston, it was about an hour later, and by then our group was really distraught. When Father Petti found us I believe he wanted to scold us, but he didn't. Instead, he took us to this wonderful restaurant in Little Italy. We had a marvelous dinner. It consisted of five courses of the most wonderful food I had ever eaten. It was one of the most fabulous times of my life.

Father Petti was an extraordinary pastor; in fact, the street at the end of the church near the rectory (at the 3600 block of Claremont Street) is named after him. In his broken English, Father Petti was able to get the whole neighborhood involved in the church. Uncle Mimi was the person who had the street named after Father Petti.

When Father Petti came here from Italy, he could not speak any English. Grandmother Annarella helped him by cooking for him, familiarizing him with the neighborhood, and introducing him to the people who lived in Highlandtown. He appreciated everything she did for him.

He formed a choir at church because, as he would always tell us, "The more you sing, the closer you will get to God." We would practice and practice, and finally we became quite good. He had a way about him that no one ever minded doing anything for him.

The nun who taught me in the fifth grade, Sister Mary, asked me to help her before and after class. I would go to school early to help her prepare her daily lessons. She would take me with her wherever she had to go, and we developed a close bond. She was from Ohio, and she would tease me and say Cleveland was going to win the World Series because she knew how much I loved the Baltimore Orioles. We would go back and forth with this all of the time.

There were only classes up to the fifth grade in the old days when Dad and his brothers and sisters attended school because they had to go to work to help support their family. So when we went to school, the sixth grade class was actually held in someone's house on Claremont Street; seventh grade was held in the back part of the choir loft in church, which also doubled as our school library. First grade and kindergarten were held in someone's house on Pratt Street. Of course, the classes were all within one block of school so that we could all go home for lunch.

Our eighth-grade class was held in a house on Conkling Street right across the street from the church. The eighth-grade nun, Sister Enus, was such a comedian. She was a short, sweet little lady, and all the kids liked her. She would say something funny, and then she would clap her hands together and say, "Okay children wipe-a-your face." She would make this gesture like wiping her face, and then she would go behind the portable blackboard. This would make us laugh so hard that we could not stop; we were hysterical with laughter at this point. She wanted us to come to attention afterward, so she could get on with the class, but it was difficult for the class to stop laughing.

After we came back from lunch one day, there were two boys who were fooling around. We were in such a confined area we had to form two lines, one for the boys, and one for the girls. While these boys were clowning around, one of them did not believe the other one had a knife; he thought he was only kidding and that he was only holding a pen behind his back. The boy backed into the knife, and he was accidentally stabbed. Sister Enus was running all around trying to help the boy, and she told someone to call an ambulance. The police came and questioned every one of us to find out what had happened. When everyone told them the same story, they did not press charges against the boy who had the knife. The police were a lot different back then. They knew the neighborhood and the people who lived in the neighborhood where they patrolled, and the police knew the two boys in question were not bad boys. Both of the boys were from good Italian, Catholic families.

Sister Enus tried to make the atmosphere more serious after this. We all had to be on our best behavior and do our class work. But even after the stabbing incident, Sister Enus made our last year before graduating from elementary school a little lighthearted.

First Bike Ride

As time went by, I started developing into a young lady. I had discovered boys! But I was only trying to have fun. I did not know anything about the "birds and the bees" then. One afternoon in October, I was outside playing with my friends, when one of the boys from school came up to me and asked me if I wanted to go for a ride on his bike. I'd never had a bike. Dad could not afford expensive toys for us because he had four children to support. If Dad bought a bike for one of us, he would have to buy one for all of us.

Curious about the experience, I jumped on the boy's bike to go for a ride. He was so cute; he had blonde hair and blue eyes, and he was the smartest boy in my class. His name was Louis. As I jumped on the bar that is in the middle of the boy's bike, I hurt myself. After a while, I went in the house to go to the bathroom, and I saw blood on my panties. I thought, "Oh my God, I hurt myself, when I jumped onto the boy's bike." I took off my panties and I threw them in the trash, because the next day was our big field trip at school and I certainly did not want to miss that. I went back outside and played some more with my friends until it was time to eat dinner. When I came inside, I hurried upstairs to see if the bleeding had stopped, and to my surprise, it had become worse. I was a nervous wreck; I thought I was going to die. I decided that after dinner I would tell Mom. I was only ten years old and I had no idea what was happening to me.

After dinner, I told Mom I had something to tell her, and it was extremely important. We went up to my room and I told her about all I had done, and I thought I was going to die. Before she told me I was having my period, she told me, "You have become a woman now, and if you kiss a boy you will have a baby." I had already kissed Louis; was I going to have a baby?

I realize that Mom tried to keep her composure and not laugh at me as she told me these things because I am sure this was very difficult for her. She had to tell the nun at school, because we were all going on our field trip in the morning. The nun had to come to the bathroom with me and make sure I was okay. I was extremely humiliated; I just wanted to put my head in the toilet, I was so embarrassed.

Mom treated me great during this time, because I suffered with such severe stomach pains that I would double over; it was horrible. There was no medication to help you then. The doctor did not believe me when I complained about menstrual pains. He told me it was all in my head. I would just hug Mom's body next to mine and the warmth of her stomach would make me feel wonderful. I will never forget how warm and comforting she was to me then. On the first day of my period, I would be terribly sick; I would throw up for two days. It was so bad Mom would keep me home from school because I could not keep anything on my stomach. I believe this was the reason why I was so thin. I could not eat for days. Because I was sickly, Dad would always say "An apple a day keeps the doctor away," another one of his favorite expressions. Being a man, he did not know how to address the subject because it was very personal. In those days, fathers never talked about such things with their daughters. It was not the proper thing to do.

I was also the first one in my class to develop breasts. I was so embarrassed; I tried to hide myself. All the boys in school would point at me and laugh, which made me even feel more self-conscious. Mom took me up to Eastern Avenue to buy some bras (like a triple-A cup). No one else in my class had developed breasts yet. When Mom got me the bras, I used to put them on first, and then I would put an undershirt on, and then a slip, and then my blouse, and a sweater over all of that, so no one could see that I had breasts. I was bashful and shy then. I was young and naïve; only ten and had no idea what was in store for me.

The Carnival

Every summer at the end of the school year the church put on a carnival. One night at the carnival, my friend Louis asked me if I wanted to go for a ride on his bike. I said yes, of course, and away he took me through the streets of Highlandtown. He would go faster than lightning. It scared me, but I never questioned him because I thought he knew what he was doing because he was so intelligent. I really liked him a lot. He always came over to my house to see me. I believe that he really cared for me. In fact, I think he was my soul mate because I never found anyone who cared for me as much as he did.

One day, Louis was riding his bike near the railroad tracks by Lombard and Haven streets in Highlandtown. The tracks were at the crest of a hill and he always tried to peddle really fast over them. But on this fateful day he came up over the railroad tracks too fast, flew up in the air, and landed on his head. The accident left him brain dead and he died shortly afterward. This was something I could not comprehend: how could such a wonderful person die so young?

Louis's funeral was the first one I ever attended for someone my own age, and everyone in my class was distraught. I believe I lost the true love of my life. If this tragic situation had not happened to him, we would be together today.

Working the Carnival

All of my relatives worked the carnival for Father Petti. Grandmother Annarella and Aunt Mary worked the fried dough stand. They would go to church early in the afternoon and start preparing the dough. Most of the older ladies in the neighborhood, along with Grandmother and Aunt Mary, hovered over the fried dough during the heat of the summer, and they would work until late in the evening. But the entire neighborhood came out to buy it because it was the best fried dough in town.

Uncle Mimi and Uncle Fritz worked the gambling wheel. Uncle Fritz loved Aunt Lena so, and he would do anything she asked him to do, such as going to church and attending its functions. He also loved Father Petti. Father Petti was the one who got Uncle Fritz to become a Catholic. Father Petti could get anyone to do anything that he asked them to do. Aunt Lena would walk the streets of the carnival and sell chances. She was the most aggressive of Dad's siblings. She made a lot of money for the church, and she was also extremely generous to the church.

Mom baked cakes for the carnival and worked the cake stand, where you could purchase a ticket for a chance to win the cakes. We would go over to her stand and try to win back the cakes that she had baked.

There were rides of all kinds—a Ferris wheel, a merry-go-round, and even pony rides—and all kinds of food, including meatball sandwiches and sausage, pepper, and onion sandwiches, too. There were plenty of fun activities for everyone. The whole neighborhood turned out because they knew how much fun the carnival was. The church was the community's lifeline because it brought everything and everyone together.

Our Easter Celebration

Every Easter Aunt Lena had a family reunion. She invited all of her brothers and sisters and their children. The day started off early in the morning with a special Mass offered for Grandmom and Grandpop at Our Lady of Pompei Church. Aunt Lena rented a hall where everyone would gather after Mass. She prepared all of the food and bought the drinks for this huge gathering. She spent weeks preparing her fabulous sauce and meatballs and buying all of the supplies she needed for the event. All the aunts and uncles helped her bring everything together. The women brought baked goods. Uncle Pat brought a huge salad tossed with oil and vinegar, salt and pepper. He told us, "It's all in the mixing." He mixed the huge salad with his large hands, until all the ingredients were all over the lettuce. Everyone looked forward to the wonderful reunions.

When the reunion started, we already knew all of our aunts and uncles, of course, but we did not know all the children and grandchildren of our cousins. So the annual reunions allowed us to get to know our extended family. We danced, ate, drank, laughed, and had fun all day. What a great party Aunt Lena would prepare for us every year.

More than 170 relatives would attend the party. Aunt Lena was the one person who seemed to get her strength from being around her family. She thrived on this day. She always wanted us to be a close-knit family.

The Amazing Aunt Lena

Aunt Lena worked for the same company all of her life. She started working for the Raleigh Clothing Company as a switchboard operator at the age of eighteen, when she was young and naïve. By the time she retired at age eighty-two, she had become the treasurer of the company. Raleigh was a subsidiary of a New York firm with the same name. When she first started to work for the company, she didn't know the company was linked to racketeering. The company did not want labor unions moving into their ranks, but Jacob Shapiro, who was related to one of the owners, brought in Lepke Buchalter, the infamous Jewish mobster and head of the notorious mafia hit squad Murder, Inc. Buchalter convinced the owners to let labor unions into their company. While Aunt Lena worked for the company, the Feds under J. Edgar Hoover and Thomas E. Dewey raided Raleigh Clothing Company, took all of their files, and arrested the secretary. Aunt Lena was devastated; she didn't understand what was happening.

Dewey claimed that Raleigh Clothing Company was involved with garment racketeering in New York. Because of Dewey's perseverance in convicting Lepke Buchalter, it elevated his notoriety and enabled him to run as a Republican candidate for President of the United States. He did not win; in fact, Dewey lost twice: once to Franklin D. Roosevelt and then to Harry S. Truman.

When the Baltimore subsidiary closed and workers moved to the New York offices, Aunt Lena decided not to go. However, the owners realized they needed Aunt Lena to take care of their books because she was so excellent with numbers. She kept the company in the black for many years, so they made her an offer she could not refuse—an apartment in Manhattan and train fare back to Baltimore every weekend—so Aunt Lena moved to New York.

Aunt Lena invited us to come and see her in New York. We could stay at her place, see New York during the day, and go out to dinner in the evening with her.

Every weekend, Uncle Fritz picked Aunt Lena up from the train station and she spent Friday evening eating crabs and drinking beer with Uncle Fritz's family. But on Saturday and Sunday, she would be eating pasta and drinking beer with her family. She loved being with us. After her fantastic weekend at home, Uncle Fritz took her back to the train station for another week of work in New York City. This commute continued until she retired at age eighty in 1999.

The Three Aunt Marys

I had three Aunt Mary's in my life. One Aunt Mary was Mom's sister, who was very religious. Another Aunt Mary was Mom's brother's wife, who lived in New Jersey. The third Aunt Mary was Dad's sister, who was the most fabulous gardener. She had every flower imaginable in her garden. She had the ability to make anything grow. She was the original green thumb. One day I asked her what her secret was, and she simply said, "Miracle Gro."

Miracle Gro Aunt Mary was married to Uncle Alex for eighty–two years, and they had five children. Aunt Mary devoted all of her time to taking care of her family. She was also a professional seamstress because back then it was more economical to make your own clothes. She made some money to help support her family from altering other people's clothes. She was also involved at Our Lady of Pompei, helping out because her mother was always at church helping out—a custom passed down by my grandmother to all of her children. Uncle Alex was for many years the president of a building and loan company in Highlandtown called La Carona. His company helped finance practically everyone's home in Highlandtown.

Top: Eighth grade graduating
class of Our Lady of Pompei
School in front of Our Lady
of Pompei Church, June 1955.
Right: Aunt Lena and Uncle
Fritz, April 1950. Below: Peachy,
Phyllis, and Clara at Our Lady of
Pompei Church, May 1948.

Seven: A Teenaged Italian

*G*randmother Annarella would spend the whole entire summer in Atlantic City. Dad wanted to be with his mother, but he was always fearful of spending money to have a good time. Living through the Depression, it was driven into his head since he was a young boy to save, save, save. But when his sister, Lena, said, "Come on, Boh, let's take a trip; we can all go to Atlantic City," he made up his mind immediately to go to Atlantic City. We followed Aunt Lena and Uncle Fritz because Dad had never been there. In fact, he had never left Baltimore before.

When we arrived, we met my grandmother who arranged for us to stay in a huge boarding house that had a community bathroom, kitchen, and wash facilities. I believe every elderly Italian lady from Highlandtown spent their whole summer there because they had virtually disappeared from the neighborhood and I saw so many of them there.

This was not really a vacation for Mom, who still had to cook, clean, and wash clothes. While we were there, Mom would make her famous spaghetti and meatballs. It was a dish that would stay with you for a long while, which meant we asked for food less often. After all, she was "supposed" to be on vacation. We helped her put the meal together; because we knew the more we helped her, the faster we would be able to go on the boardwalk and get on the rides.

Mom's Meatball Recipe:
5 lbs. ground round
3 eggs beaten well
5 tbsp. milk
1-½ tbsp. oregano
2 tbsp. parsley
1 ½ tbsp. salt
10 pcs. basil, diced

5 tsp. crushed garlic
1/4 tsp. black pepper
8 slices white bread, diced.

Beat the eggs well, and add the milk. Then add the meat, all of the seasoning, and bread. Mix thoroughly until all of the ingredients are blended together. Preheat the oven to 350 degrees, and roll the meatballs while you are waiting for the oven to reach the right temperature. Place the meatballs on a tray, and bake in the oven for about twenty to thirty minutes. When they are finished cooking, place the meatballs in the sauce. Serves 6.

Mom's Favorite Store

Before heading up to Atlantic City, Mom and Dad went to her favorite store on "The Avenue," Epstein's, to buy a bathing suit. She never needed one until the family decided to go to the beach. My parents never took a vacation because their strict up-bringing made them afraid to enjoy some pleasures in life.

Dad would say, "Phil, you keep this store in business because you are here every week," and Mom would just laugh. Mom loved Epstein's because the store had everything from men's and women's clothing to furniture, rugs, curtains, baby clothes, kitchen appliances, and the most wonderful policy: lay-away! Dad's pay had to go a long way, so Mom stretched it as far as she could.

Our Day at the Beach

We went to the beach every day in Atlantic City. Mom packed a lunch, Dad rented a huge umbrella, and he brought an old blanket so we could all relax and sun ourselves on the sand.

One day, Mom went up to the boardwalk with Grandmom Annarella and Aunt Lena. She told Dad, "Take care of Rosie because she is still a baby." Rosie had developed a mind of her own, however, even though she was young. Dad was reading the paper, and my brothers and I were making sand castles. We all had forgotten about Rosie. She was there, and then all of a sudden she was gone. When mom came back from the boardwalk; she cried, "Oh my goodness, where's the baby?"

Mom was a basket case. Dad was a mess. He went down to the water pacing back and forth looking for Rosie and smoking one cigarette after another. He thought for sure that she had drowned. He was totally distraught. Johnny was consoling Mom, and Vincent and I took off running looking up and down the beach for Rosie. We asked many people if they had seen a little girl in a pink bathing suit.

Finally, someone told us there was an area up ahead on the beach where they kept lost children. We found a gigantic playpen full of lost children and in the playpen was my little sister, Rosie. I swept her up and kissed her. Vince and I were so excited that we found our sister that we forgot to thank the people for finding her. Vince and I took Rosie and ran all the way back to Mom and Dad, who were absolutely frantic by this time. Mom grabbed her and held her like there was no tomorrow. Everyone was relieved that Rosie was all right. My parents would not let her out of their sight after this episode. Rosie told us she went to throw something away in the trash can, and then she could not find her way back to where we were. Little Rosie was very frightened, and after this incident she was attached to Mom's hip. She would not leave Mom's side and Mom did not want her to, either.

Clara and her mother and their whole family were also at the boarding house. Down the street from the boarding house was a nightclub. Clara told me that Dean Martin and Jerry Lewis were going to be there later on in the evening. She said, "Come on Peach, if we are the first in line, we will be the first to see them when they go into the club." Clara and I stood in line behind a huge rope waiting to see Dean Martin and Jerry Lewis arrive at the club. I believe we were there for two hours before they showed up. We were so close to them, we could have touched them. This was the highlight of my stay in Atlantic City. What a great experience it was to see these two great movie stars in person.

First Pair of Jeans

I had finally persuaded Mom to buy me a pair of jeans that really fit me. She would always buy me size twelve, and say, "You'll grow into them," when I was really only a size three. Wow, did I feel great wearing the jeans; they fit me just right and showed off all of my curves.

One time Dad asked me to go to the store on "The Avenue" to buy him cigarettes. On the way back home, I ran into a friend from school. I was one block away from our home standing on the street corner under a big street light talking to a boy from school when Dad came looking for me. You see, it was 9:30 P.M. and he was wondering what had happened to me. When he saw me talking to a boy, he said, "Get home, girl." When I got into the house, he said, "Take those pants off girl." He ripped my new jeans (you know how sturdy they are made) from the bottom all the way around the crotch to the other end. He said later, "I am cutting your hair when you go to sleep." He said, "Your long hair is what attracts boys to you." He was afraid something bad was going to happen to me. He was terribly overprotective. I was afraid he would do what he said and cut my hair, but I am sure Mom stopped him. Mom was always my protector, as she was for all of us.

There had been some killings of young girls in Baltimore at this time, and Dad was afraid that this might happen to me. The person or persons who did this were never caught, which made it more of a concern to Dad. Although he was a tough Italian father, Dad would not hurt a fly unless you did something to his family. He was strong on the outside and soft on the inside.

Whenever Dad "went on the warpath," as we called it, about my going out, Mom would stand in between him and me and say, "Carmen, if you touch her, I swear I will leave you." I would run upstairs and try to lock myself in the bathroom. If he wanted he could have come after me, but Mom always threatened to leave him if he did, and then he would stop. There were many times in the kitchen though, where he would push the table in the corner and catch me in between the kitchen sink and the stove. Then Mom would again say, "Carmen, I swear, if you touch her, I will leave you," and then he would stop.

I had reached my teen years, and I started to rebel against my parents. I thought I was all grown up. I had a lot of living to do, and I was going to put all of this living in during my teen years. I was always Dad's little girl, but after Rosie was born, it was all about her. I was hurt that they took all their affection off me and put it on Rosie. I became the middle child, the forgotten one. I went into seclusion, feeling like I was left out of the loop. Vincent was the first-born, and Dad had him doing projects with him every Saturday. They would either be in the garage or in the basement or working on the car. Johnny was Mom's favorite; he was constantly near her, because he was too small to help Dad with his special projects. Then there was Rosie, and she was the special one, because she was the baby.

I thought I had lost all of Dad's affection. I was bewildered because I was entering my teen years. I started to "hang" with my girl-friends. I thought my friends were everything, but on the contrary, as I grew older, I found out my parents were the most important people in my life and that they cared about me more than anything.

A Broken Leg

Mom had finally gotten a job at Pompei church again. She would have lots of little chores for us to do after school; mine was ironing or helping with the cooking. (The first time I started to peel an egg-plant, my hands turned purple. I was so frightened that I ran to the neighbor's house crying about my purple hands, but Ms. Irene said it was only from the eggplant and I'd be okay.) Johnny watched my sister Rosie. Vince would run errands.

One day, Vince had to go to Wetzelberger's, a store just one block from our house. It was Mom's lifesaver store and she would send us there at least four or five times a day after school. We would go and get bread, and when we came home, she would say, "Oh my good-ness, I need potatoes." When we came back, again she would say, "Oh my goodness, I forgot the onions." When we came back home, she would say, "I need lettuce for the salad." This would go on and on until it was time for dinner, when all along she was doing this on purpose to keep us busy while she was preparing dinner.

Once while I was ironing, my two brothers were in the living room playing with Rosie, tickling her, and watching TV. All of a sudden, Rosie fell from the couch onto the floor. Just this little fall broke her leg. You might have thought the end of the world had come because we were all punished. Mom had just gotten her old job back, and was trying to make a little spending money, but Dad said she had to quit her job. Dad told Mom, "If you had been home this would not have happened to Rosie." There went Mom's extra spending money.

I had a date to go out that weekend, but everything was cancelled, all because my sister broke her leg. Dad wanted to keep us protected all of our lives. He wanted to make sure nothing bad would happen to any one of us, and when something did, we all had to stay together and regroup.

The House on Claremont

On Sundays we went for a drive to visit one of my aunts or uncles. While driving around town, Mom would look at houses thinking maybe we needed a new place as the children grew older. She wanted us to have our own rooms. Now, as I look back on everything, I do not know when my parents ever had time to themselves because we were always with them.

We would go looking for a new house almost every Sunday, but because Dad was so conservative, we never moved. He was concerned about payments on a new house, and if he got sick or if anything happened to him, we would not be able to make ends meet. He had already paid for our home, and all of the houses Mom went to look at then are in bad neighborhoods today. If we had moved to one of those homes, we would have had to move again, and I would not be living in my parents' home today.

On the way back from these Sunday drives, Dad would sing his famous song to us: "There's no place like home, there's no place like home." And you know what? There never was any place like home.

The house at 3510 Claremont Street will be in the same family for seventy-five years in 2013.

Brother Johnny

In the summer, my girlfriend Lucy and I would sit on the front steps and play jacks, with Lucy winning as usual. A boy came up to us and he put gum in my hair just to be mean. Around the corner came Johnny (he had been playing baseball with his friend Jimmy who lived across the alley from us). He grabbed the boy and pushed him up against our house. He told him if he ever hurt me again, he would really take care of him, and Johnny was little then.

Johnny played with Jimmy all the time. They were best friends. With the help of Dad, Johnny made a wooden crate and attached his rollerskates to it so that the boys could have a soapbox derby right on Claremont Street. Johnny loved baseball so much because Dad would take him to some of the Orioles games. Even though they had to sit in the bleachers, they still had great times at the ball games. Dad also made Johnny a toy wagon from scratch, and then Johnny and Vince would go through the neighborhood, collect all the old newspapers, and take them to the recycling center. They would collect the large sum of sixty-five cents for 500 pounds of newspaper.

Johnny had a round face with a warm smile. When he was young, he had light brown hair and was a little on the heavy side. His friend Jimmy was built just like him. Johnny was such a happy-go-lucky guy, but he was also shy. People would call him "Quiet John." He might have been quiet, but he was strong just like Dad. Johnny had many friends who are still his friends today.

One of his friends sold Christmas trees at a store that was right around the corner from our house. We all called him "Joe Christmas Tree." Johnny hung out in the store all the time with his friends. It was just a neighborhood soda shop, but everyone from the neighborhood went there. Johnny liked the woman who owned the store, even though she was older than he was.

One time when Johnny was small, he got hungry during a visit to Aunt Jenny's. Johnny asked her, "Do you want me to have a jelly sandwich?"

She said, "Johnny, you can have anything you want."

After this funny episode we kidded him all the time. What a great guy Johnny was. He supported us in anything we wanted to do in our lives. He was also extremely intelligent. After he graduated from high school, he attended the University of Baltimore. He started to work for a meat packing company in Highlandtown called Esskay. His employers liked Johnny so much they paid his way through college. It was a huge meat packing plant, and Johnny worked his way up the corporate ladder until he was the Credit Manager (all while attending night school at the UB). He worked there for twenty-three years, and he would come home for lunch every day, and don't you know that Mom would have lunch ready for him. The two of them grew so close through the years Johnny watched over her, which he did for a long period of time. Johnny loved Mom so much, he did not want her to be left alone and Mom in return did everything for him including ironing his shorts. John grew up to be the strongest person in our family, so tall and handsome and very smart when it came to finances (he took care of Mom's finances).

Later John became the Branch Credit Manager and Corporate Credit Manager of a huge food supply company called U. S. Foods. Everyone at work loved him because he treated everyone fairly. Company management recognized his experience and talent in the Credit and Collection Department, and that he had such a way about him, that they would send him all over to collect money that was owed. He could talk you into whatever he wanted you to do, and then he would show you his warm smile, and you just could not refuse him. Johnny was another strong influence who helped to guide me during my life. He tried to point me in the right direction, and he was always on my side.

Right: "There's no place like home," 3510 Claremont Street after the formstone facade was added, 1973. Below: Family vacation in Atlantic City with Vince, Carmen, Johnny (back) and Phyllis, Peachy, and Rose (front), 1955. Lower right: Johnny DiPietro, October 1985.

Eight: Old Patterson High

After graduation from Pompei, almost everyone from High-landtown went to Patterson Park High School. What a social change this was, from having the nuns telling you what was right and what was wrong to being basically on our own in public school. The teachers were professional, but it was a big difference from Catholic school. The first year in high school just flew by. We had a lot of adjustments to make, one was changing classes all day long. Then we had a lunch period, where you could either buy your lunch or bring it from home. There was time to spend together with your classmates and talk.

We also had assemblies every week where we were taught grooming lessons. The teachers would put on shows to make us see how comical we looked in the clothes that we wore. During this time, you were either a "square," which meant you wore thick bobby socks and oxford shoes and dressed Ivy League, or you were a "drape," wearing jeans and a white shirt with the sleeve rolled up where you stuck your cigarettes. These shows made you realize how comical you appeared to other people. So eventually, we got the hint and changed our way of dressing.

By the time I reached tenth grade we started to act more sensibly. Everything was so different, and the teachers were fabulous. A new experience came with physical education. We all had to change into our gym clothes in front of one another. I was not used to this, and it was very awkward for me.

The Buddy Deane Show

During my teenage years, there were two great shows that came on TV after school. One was the "Howdy Doody Show," and the other was the "Buddy Deane Show." Vince and I would argue over which one to watch because they came on at the same time on different channels. Mom would have to separate us and make us do something for her like going to the store several times or helping her with dinner or ironing clothes for her.

I had become a good dancer from all the dances held at church and school, and I won several contests. Clara and I had gotten tickets to go to the Buddy Deane Show where they awarded prizes to the best dancers. We would go there to try to win the prizes. Often, I would win the contests and walk away with all the prizes. One time, a group of girls I did not know were jealous of my success. After the show, they waited outside to pick a fight with me. I never knew how to fight, but needless to say, I tried to do the best I could. Finally, the cops came and broke up the fight. No one really got hurt. Clara and I went home as if nothing had happened; if our parents had found out, we would never be allowed to go on the Buddy Deane Show again.

Cousin Clara

Clara and I were inseparable. Clara was a beautiful girl, short with brown hair and a round face and brown eyes. People called us the "buckle and the strap" because we would appear everywhere together. Every time I wanted to go to a dance or a party, Clara's mother, Aunt Lucy, would be the go-between. She was Dad's cousin and would say to him, "Come on, Boh, (Dad's nickname) let the girls go out. They only want to dance and have fun." He would let me go, although being a natural worry-wort he was very skeptical.

Clara and I loved going to the movies also. We were both romantic fools, and we were living in the Doris Day/Rock Hudson era where everything was sweet and rosy. We saw many movies together because movies were affordable enough that our parents could send us. Besides, Mom was a hopeless romantic herself, although she grew up in the Rudolph Valentino era.

Clara and I went to the movies to see *Kismet*, where Vic Damone sang "Stranger in Paradise" and I thought that one day I would meet someone like this. I was so young and full of expectations of having a life with someone to love me like Vic Damone loved Ann Blyth.

One time Clara and I went to the movie theater to see an Elvis Presley movie. I thought he was just gorgeous, and the way he moved was unreal. Some critics tried to blackball him from appearing in public. Music critics and parents all over made petitions to stop disc jockeys from playing his records on the radio. People said, "If our children listen to Elvis's music, he will make our girls crazy." Everyone was overprotective then.

When we went to the movies to see Elvis, I could not contain myself; my hormones were "all shook up." I had never seen anyone move like he did given the sheltered life I lived. The usher (yes, there were ushers then) came down the aisle and warned me if I did not stop screaming he would be forced to remove me from the movie theatre. I tried to behave myself, but my hormones were kicking in high gear, and I could not help but let out a few more screams. Down the aisle the usher came. "Out!" he said. "That is just about enough from you, young lady." He ushered me straight out of the theater.

During my sophomore year, I met a boy who looked exactly like Elvis, but his name was Butch. He was short with black hair and side burns just like Elvis. We would spend hours on the phone talking to each other, and I thought that I had fallen in love. He showed so much interest in me and I was totally infatuated with him. He was my first real boyfriend.

Connie, a friend who lived across the street from me, told me to join all of the different activities in school. She said that it would help me to acquire extra points in school. So I joined as many activities as possible. Connie was short and cute and had long black hair and was also from an Italian family. Because of my busy schedule full of activities, I could not spend much time with Butch. He became jealous so eventually we broke up.

Teachers at Patterson

I took up office work in school because Mom told me that is what she did when she went to school, and I wanted to be just like her. One of my favorite teachers was Mr. Kolb. He helped me with shorthand all through school. It was very difficult for me to get used to all the symbols and pen strokes used in shorthand. He would allow me to come in early and do extra-curricular work. Mr. Mainen also helped me with my stenography. With their help I overcome the challenges.

Mr. Ewell, the math teacher, also accommodated me. I could not comprehend math at all, but Mr. Ewell gave me extra work to take home so I could improve my skills.

Meanwhile, a romance blossomed between our beautiful typing teacher, Miss Francis, and the music teacher, Mr. Wroblewski. We were mesmerized by their developing love story from the day Mr. Wroblewski presented Miss Francis with a beautiful engagement ring. Being teenagers, we were impressed by such a romantic gesture. The two teachers are still together today. They have four children, and three of them are doctors.

The History Adventure

I joined the United Nations Club because I loved history and I wanted to learn as much as possible about it. We were supposed to go on a field trip to New York City and visit the U.N. building. I could hardly wait to go. Unfortunately, I missed the last meeting before the trip because I was ill, and the time of our trip had been changed, but no one informed me. Mom woke me up early in the morning to go on my trip. I took a cab to the train station, thinking I would meet my other classmates there, but to my surprise, no one from my class was there. I did not know what to do.

While I was at the train station, there was a group of younger children with their teacher. I began to talk to the teacher, and I asked her where she was going. She told me she was going to the U.N. building, the same trip that I was supposed to be going on. She invited me to come with them. She said, "I could use your help with the children." Having already purchased the ticket for the trip, I went on the train to New York City with perfect strangers and had a grand time. The children loved me because I was older, and I treated them as my equals.

When we went into the U.N. building, there was a big statue of a man with no clothes on. I am sure it is some special art exhibit, but at this age, I was embarrassed, and so were the little children. They were all laughing and pointing to the statue. We toured the building and sat in on some of the meetings. Afterwards, we ate in a big restaurant then went back to the train station to go home. I had such a wonderful time with the nice strangers.

My teacher, Mrs. Baldwin, had rescheduled our trip for one hour later than what I was told, so my class was one hour behind me all day long. When I returned to history class the next week and told the teacher what had happened, she could not believe what an experience I had. The teacher from the other school gave me her phone number to verify my story. She gave me a great reference, and therefore, I received my credits for going on the trip and I even got extra credits because I had escorted the younger students to New York.

I was involved in so many school activities and sports that I really did not have time for a boyfriend. Connie told me that I could receive letters for all of the different achievements to sew on my sweater. The more letters you received, the more impressive it looked on your sweater. I received seven letters all together.

The Junior Prom

Vince got me a date with one of his classmates for the junior prom, and because he was one of my brother's friends, I was allowed to go out with him. We had a great time at the prom; we danced all night long. But when it came time for him to take me home, he pulled the car up to my house and started groping me all over. I was startled and could not believe what was happening. I do not know how I did it, but I got him off of me and ran into the house. I never told anyone because I did not want Vince to get upset.

Managing a Campaign

In my junior year, we had to elect a class president for our senior year. I was the campaign manager for Gail who was running for president, and she won. I made all different sorts of slogans and passed them out around school to try to get the students to vote for my candidate. She was an incredibly intelligent person, and she was actually the most qualified for the job. I loved politics even when

I was young, and after the tremendous victory, I wanted to have a party. I rented Uncle Mimi's Democratic Club for the special event. I charged everyone $15 to enter, which helped pay for the rental fee and the food and sodas. However, some guys crashed the party. These things happened all the time then. When the word got out that there was a party in the neighborhood, the party crashers managed to find out where the party was, and all of a sudden all these boys who no one knew would arrive at the party. The boys almost caused a riot because they snuck beer into the party, and they did not care about anything except partying.

Before I knew what was happening, they broke the bathroom door because they were drunk. I got really upset and made everyone leave. I knew I was going to be in big trouble with Uncle Mimi and Dad. How was I ever going to explain what happened? With the help of Vince, who fixed the bathroom door, I was saved.

The Passing of My Grandparents DiPietro

My dad's father, Grandpop Gaetano, died from stomach cancer in February of 1957. He suffered so much from the pains in his stomach. My grandmother took excellent care of him through all of the agonizing pain. She helped him through the entire unbearable situation.

Although everyone was upset when Grandpop passed away, all of Grandmom's children could not understand why she had to suffer such horrible pain herself for such a long time. Grandmom Annarella died from bone cancer in March of 1959. Grandmom was such a loving, caring person that none of her children wanted to see her go through such horrible discomfort. I never saw Dad cry before, but when he came home and told Mom that his mother had died, he broke down and cried like a baby. He never forgot how his mother always looked after him during his whole life. She always took up for him during his early days, and her passing tremendously upset him.

Top: Patterson Park High School at Ellwood Avenue and Lombard Street, 1939. Right: Carol Smith, Peachy DiPietro, and Clara Tana at Carol's home on East Avenue, 1960.

Nine: The Famous Uncle Mimi

*U*ncle Mimi, Dad's brother, was the local politician from our neighborhood. He helped everyone out and made sure Highlandtown, where he grew up, was taken care of. He was loved and respected for all of the good deeds he did for his constituents.

He became involved in politics because he could speak Italian, as did most of the neighborhood. He translated for them, and when he found out what they needed, Uncle Mimi told the precinct executive. Most of the people who lived in Highlandtown when he was younger were Republicans, but by 1930 everyone in the neighborhood turned Democratic. Uncle Mimi became president of the United Democratic Club, which was right down the street from his home. When Tommy D'Alesandro, Jr., became Mayor of Baltimore City, Uncle Mimi became his messenger boy, and this is how he got started in politics. He was appointed to the City Council in 1966, the year before Tommy D'Alesandro, III, was elected mayor (the DiPietros and the D'Alesandros came from the same Abruzzi area in Italy northwest of Rome).

One politician decided he was going to put a landfill in Highlandtown on Highland Avenue and Monument Street. I called Uncle Mimi and asked him if he could keep this from happening to our neighborhood. I said, "Uncle Mimi, they are going to dump trash in our backyard. Please do something to help us." I have no idea what he did, but with his expertise, this land is now used for storing all of the props used for city activities and this location never become a landfill. When he called someone from the city to do whatever he needed, everyone paid attention to him.

Everyone knew if you went to Mimi DiPietro with a problem, he would take care of it for you. He would make you come into his office, and the first thing he would ask you was, "Do you vote?" If you said no, he made you walk across the street to the Voter Registration Board where his friend Gene Raynor worked. He said, "First you register, then come back and see me and I'll see what I can do to help you."

He would have a three-way conversation going on in his office in no time at all. He got right down to the facts and found out who was responsible for whatever the person wanted Uncle Mimi to fix, and with the snap of his fingers the problem was solved. One of the most important things my uncle taught me was to make sure you get the name of the person to whom you are speaking and document it. Therefore, if you had any trouble, you would have the name of the person you talked to so that you could go back and question the person about why the job was not done.

Uncle Mimi's Good Deeds

One day one of my neighbors, Margaret, who lived across the street from church, called my uncle for help. Her daughter was getting married, but there had been a blizzard and extremely deep snow covered the street. The bride was unable to make it across the street to the church, and both the mother and daughter were in a panic. After making all of the plans for the wedding, the snow was about to ruin it. Margaret called Uncle Mimi and said, "Oh, Mimi, my daughter is getting married, and she can't even make it across the street." In no time at all, he had city workers plow and shovel the whole street, up and down and in front of Our Lady of Pompei, and even the church steps. The woman looked outside to see what was going on. When the worker saw her, he came over to her and asked her, "Hey lady! Who died?" This is how much power my uncle had. He got anything repaired that the neighborhood needed. When Uncle Mimi called someone to repair something for his constituents, it was immediately and correctly repaired.

Stopping Traffic

I remember the time when the people who lived on Lombard Street asked Uncle Mimi to stop the big trucks from driving down Lombard. The trucks were damaging the foundations of homes along the street and the neighbors were extremely upset. One night he stood in the middle of Lombard Street with Mayor Schaefer and other councilmen and neighbors and made the trucks take another route. The TV news showed up with cameras rolling and the reporters interviewed Uncle Mimi, who always provided them with colorful comments. In the end, Uncle Mimi got a bill passed through the City Council to re-route truck traffic on Lombard Street.

He did not go to college because his parents, my grandparents, were poor. He had to go to work to help support his family, but this did not stop his ambitions. He was elected to six four-year terms on the City Council, and he served his constituents well for many years. Because he did not go past the sixth grade, he did not use proper English, but it did not matter because he would always get the job done. A long article about his life appeared in the *Baltimore Sun* when Uncle Mimi died in 1994 at the age of 89.

The Beginning of the Inner Harbor

I believe Mayor William Donald Schaefer was the best mayor we ever had. He was the person who initiated the reconstruction of the Inner Harbor. He visited Boston to see how their harbor area was restored with a beautiful aquarium. He was amazed to see all the people visiting it. Schaefer imagined all the revenue that was being brought into the city of Boston, which gave him the idea to build an aquarium in Baltimore. When he came back home, he told the City Council that he wanted to build an aquarium, but he received much opposition. He had the vision and foresight to see the potential that would come out of revitalizing the Inner Harbor.

Mayor Schaefer turned the rat-infested harbor's edge into the dazzling showplace that it is today. Mayor Schaefer was the only person who promoted the construction of the National Aquarium in Baltimore. He wanted the aquarium to be built by a certain date, and he said, "I will dress up in an old fashioned swim suit and jump into a small wading pool at the Inner Harbor." He did this to show the people of Baltimore how committed he was to this major project. Before he did this, he asked his friend Gene Raynor if he thought it was a good idea. Mr. Raynor told him that he did not think it was. Still, the photographers took a picture of him in the swimsuit holding a rubber ducky, and the picture received national attention in *Time* magazine. Mayor Schaefer told Mr. Raynor, "The next time I want to ask you for some political advice, I will do the opposite of what you tell me to do." He knew that once the National Aquarium was completed people from all over the country would come and visit it, and they have.

Thousands of people visit our lovely city to see the many different entertaining places like the National Aquarium and the Science Center and all of the stores and restaurants that are in the Inner Harbor. Mayor Schaefer had the insight to see that it would bring large amounts of revenue into the City, and it has. And as Uncle Mimi had done many times in the past, he helped Mayor Schaefer get the bill passed through the City council to provide funds to build the aquarium.

Park Benches on "The Avenue" and the Democratic Club

Another time, Uncle Mimi put park benches in the Eastern Avenue shopping district for elderly people to rest on while they were shopping. In fact, Uncle Mimi beautified the whole shopping area, arranging for the city to put red bricks all around the corners of Conkling Street and Eastern Avenue. Trees were planted by benches to provide shade. When Uncle Mimi found out the homeless were sleeping on the benches, he became furious. He went to "The Avenue" and made them get off the benches. He said, "These benches are for the people who come to Eastern Avenue to shop, not for you bums to sleep on." When he found out they were sleeping on the benches again, he had the benches removed. He wanted to keep the neighborhood clean. Uncle Mimi knew the people who lived in Highlandtown were all blue-collar workers. He did not want them to have to deal with these people while they were shopping. The trees and the red bricks are still there, but the benches are gone.

Back in 1937, Uncle Mimi started the Men's United Democratic Club and Ladies Club. He was President of the Men's Club for over sixty years. He was also the perennial ticket-leader in the First District. He made sure that alleys were cleaned and potholes were filled, and he always acquired jobs for his constituents.

Taking Care of His Brother

Uncle Mimi was committed to take care of his brother Sammy, because he had epilepsy and was developmentally disabled. Uncle Mimi had promised his mother that he would look after Sammy after she died. They lived together through the rest of their lives in the same house that belonged to his parents. Uncle Mimi took Sammy everywhere with him, and he always made sure that he was dressed well.

His sister Lena worked for the clothing company, and he called her and asked her if they could come to her place of business and get fitted for suits. They would go to church together every Sunday. He really cared about his brother because he thought that Sammy had been cheated out of a normal life.

Christopher Columbus

Then there was the time when the committee for the Columbus Day parade wanted to move the statue of Christopher Columbus from Clifton Park, which was near North Avenue and Belair Road. There was a huge parade every Columbus Day, and all of the little children had to walk in the parade. The neighborhood had been changing for years, and it was getting dangerous for the children to march in the parade. There were drugs everywhere. The people in charge of the parade came to Uncle Mimi and asked him if there was anything that he could do to help them. He came up with a plan to have the statue moved to the Inner Harbor near Little Italy. He said, "When Christopher Columbus landed in America, he landed on the water not in a park."

So the statue was moved near the water, much to the delight of parade organizers. There now stands a plaque in Little Italy right near the statue, with Uncle Mimi's name on it, stating that he was one of the people responsible for having the statue moved to its new location. The parade is now held at the Inner Harbor, where the statue stands today.

Patterson Park Rink

There is a fantastic ice skating rink bearing Uncle Mimi's name in Patterson Park. It has a huge, white dome over it to protect people from the weather because Uncle Mimi wanted children to be able to skate even if the weather was bad. There is a fireplace inside so you can come in from the cold to warm yourself. There is hot chocolate and some light food sold there also. All kinds of special events are held at the ice skating rink. A boy's ice hockey team practices there and the boys wear tee shirts and jackets that say Mimi DiPietro's Ice Rink. For a nominal fee, you can take your family there and have a fun-filled day.

Keeping the Neighborhood Clean

One of my friends, Lill, went to buy some sausage from the Roma Sausage Company, which was at Claremont and Fagley across the street from my uncle's house. Uncle Mimi was outside sweeping the sidewalks and the alleys.

She said, "Mimi, what are you doing sweeping the street?"

He told her, "If everyone would clean their pavements, alleys, and keep their own property clean, do you know how much money they would save the city? We could use this money for other projects."

Lill could not believe that the "Mayor of Highlandtown" cleaned his own property, but she was so impressed that from then on she would keep her front (actually her whole street) clean.

Election Time

I would work the polls for Uncle Mimi when he was running for City Council. I passed out pamphlets and asked people to vote for my uncle. It would make me so upset when people would not take my pamphlets because this meant they were not going to vote for him. I could not understand this at all. How could they not vote for Uncle Mimi? He did everything for the neighborhood and his constituents. He loved Highlandtown, and all he ever wanted to do was to make it a better place for all of us to live.

Going to Italy

Uncle Mimi and his sister Aunt Lena went on a trip to Italy with Father Petti and several other Our Lady of Pompei parishoners. On the trip was a woman named Frances Promutico. She had dark hair and was a little on the heavy side. She was single, as was Uncle Mimi. Frances lived one block from Uncle Mimi, and of course Uncle Mimi knew everyone in Highlandtown, but they had never met. While they were in this beautiful country of Italy, they fell in love. Uncle Mimi was so involved with his job in Baltimore that he never had time to go out on dates. He would socialize, but it would always involve politics. After spending all of these wonderful days together in Italy, they returned to Baltimore and continued their relationship. It took a beautiful trip to this romantic country to bring these two special people together. Uncle Mimi married Aunt Frances on February 13, 1966. He was 61 and she was 41.

Aunt Frances idolized Uncle Mimi and did everything for him. They were truly in love with each other. Uncle Mimi thought it was a shame that they never got together sooner because he would have loved to spend more years with Aunt Frances.

Aunt Frances's mother was a good friend of Mom's. Her name was Rose, and she was a widow. Her husband had died of a heart attack at an early age. Miss Rose was the seamstress of Highlandtown. She made all of the costumes for me and the other children in Highlandtown when we were in class plays. Miss Rose made the costume for me as Little Bo Peep (as seen on this book's cover). I can remember Mom going to Miss Rose's shop and buying different things that she needed for the house. Miss Rose would also come to our house and have coffee with Mom.

There were many, many more good deeds that my uncle did, but they are too numerous to mention. Uncle Mimi worked many long hours serving his neighborhood, and his constituents called on him for everything imaginable. Uncle Mimi thought it was such an honor to be chosen by the people to be a public servant. He was constantly there for them, and since he passed away on August 5, 1994, the neighborhood has gone down hill. It has taken more than fifteen years for Highlandtown to come back to life again.

Top left: Mimi DiPietro at work in Baltimore's City Hall, February 1978. Top right: Mimi DiPietro breaking ground for a school with Mayor Thomas D'Alesandro, Jr., 1950. Mimi and Lena DiPietro and relatives at the Trevi Fountain in Rome, Italy, 1965. During this trip, Mimi fell in love with Frances Promutico.

Ten: Brother Vince

*U*ince was extremely intelligent; he had terrific grades at Patterson High School. He knew if he did not go to college, he could not get an excellent job. Actually, both of my brothers were intelligent, and they both went to college. Vince was interested in space when he was young, and he really wanted to be an astronaut. He even wrote a book about Mars, because he discovered evidence of life on Mars while he worked at Goddard Space Center. He tried to convince people that there was life on Mars. He insisted that there was once water on Mars, but people did not believe him. They would tell him it was impossible. After he wrote the book about Mars, he went on many TV interviews to discuss Mars. He studied the reports of several other scientists, who found fossil evidence in meteorites, which have now been proven to have come from Mars.

Vince's Young Years

Vince had a friend who was a short, thin guy with light hair and glasses. His name was Albert. Vince was also short and thin, had brown hair, and wore glasses. They were both extremely intelligent, and in their early years they were both into science, astronomy, and physics.

They would build rockets in Dad's garage, take them down to Patterson Park, and fire them off. Sometimes, they would take their rockets to the school lot across the street from Grandma Annarella's house on Claremont Street and shoot them off there. They would do these projects before sunset because at this time of day most people were eating dinner. Through many years of performing experiments, they discovered the fascinating aspects of science. No one could understand their insight into outer space, because they were both far ahead of the times. They even made a home movie about space. They were into rockets, space, and many science projects before it was popular to be interested in such things.

Vincent Goes to College

I remember the time Vince went away to college at the University of Maryland in College Park, Maryland to the School of Engineering. Mom acted as if he was going away forever and she was never going to see him again. Mom's heart was broken, for her first-born was leaving home. As time went by though, she got over her depression because Vince kept coming home every weekend and bringing all his dirty clothes. She would prepare a big meal for him when he came home, and she would make lots of goodies for him to take back. She would wash his dirty clothes and make sure he had plenty of clean clothes to take back to school with him. After doing this week in and week out, she finally realized that he did not leave home after all.

The Flu

While Vince was in college, a horrible flu hit the whole state of Maryland. Johnny and Rosie were the first in our house to be hit with the flu, I am sure it was because they were the smallest, and their resistance was low. Mom took special care of them, because the news was reporting every day about how many people were getting the flu, and that some people had even died. This really commanded Mom's constant attention. She listened religiously to find out the latest developments. The TV was her link to the outside world. When the TV personalities came into our home every evening, they made us feel like they were part of our family. There was one broadcaster in particular Mom loved. He was a distinguished gentleman, and his hair was a beautiful white. He had such a way about him you could not help but love him. He was tall, thin, and extremely handsome. His name was Jerry Turner. While he was broadcasting the news on Channel 13, he made jokes that you could not help but laugh at. He would also laugh at his own jokes, and when he did this, you could not resist joining in and laughing along with him. He was such a terrific anchorman; everyone in Baltimore loved him. One of his biggest fans was Mom.

We also had the most wonderful doctor who lived a half a block from our house. Anytime any one of us was sick, we would either go to his office, which was constantly busy, or he would make a doctor's visit to our house. Imagine this, a doctor coming to your house for a visit. Could you see this happening today? The doctor was tall, thin, and wore glasses. He had light brown hair and a warm smile. He was soft spoken, which made you feel safe while you were in his care. His name was Dr. John Constantini.

While Mom was taking care of my brother and sister, she got the flu herself. Dad called Vince at college and told him not to come home this weekend, because the flu had hit our home. They were afraid if he came home, he would get sick also, and then he could not go back to school. Dad was upset when Mom became sick, because she was the one who took care of everyone. He loved her so, and he never wanted anything to happen to her. You could tell how concerned he was about her, because he was always at her bedside. Dad and I had to take care of Mom, John, Rosie, and ourselves. Finally, Dad caught it, and I was left to take care of everyone, but it was not long after this, that I caught the flu myself.

Our wonderful doctor's wife who was tall, thin, and very friendly, made a large pot of chicken soup and brought it over for all of us to eat. Can you imagine that? What a great person she was. She had four children of her own but she managed to find the time out of her busy day to make something special for our family. What a wonderful community I lived in.

Vince's First Job

My brother got a job as a lab technician, and he made the huge salary of sixty dollars a week. Vince had to give his whole paycheck to Dad, and then Dad would give him some spending money. This is what Dad had to do when he was working and living at home with his parents, and therefore he expected Vince to do the same. They had a huge argument. Vince said, "How can I ever get ahead if you take all of my pay check?" He left the house and found a place to live in Essex, and Mom was heartbroken. She cried her eyes out, and she made herself ill. Mom could not even eat because her first-born baby left home.

Johnny and I found out where Vince was staying through my cousin Freddie, and we went there to beg Vince to come home. We told him how ill Mom was over his leaving, and he had to come home before something seriously went wrong with her. Finally, Vince came back home to live, and Mom was relieved. After Dad saw how upset Mom was over Vince's leaving, he agreed that Vince could pay room and board and keep most of his paycheck.

Vince then got another job. Now he was working two jobs because he wanted to save money to buy a car. He would have to get up early in the morning, because he would have to take buses to and from both of his jobs. If he missed one of his buses, he would not get home until late in the evening. While he was working, he saved enough money for a car. Finally he met his goal; he bought Dad's big black 1950 Chevy. He was able to get back and forth from both jobs, and he did not have to wait on the corner anymore for buses during inclement weather.

The Adventures of Brother Vince

In January of 1961, Vince went into the service. He wanted to join the Air Force, but they told him there was a waiting list, so he joined the Army Reserve instead and went to boot camp. He served in the Army for six months, and when he came home from the service, he could not get one of his jobs back. At the aircraft company in Essex, they simply told him he had been laid off during the time he was away. He went back to work for the chemical company, but it was extremely dangerous. The company had exotic chemicals that Vince had to work with. He left and went to work for an electronics company.

He then found the car of his dreams. It was a red '57 Thunderbird, with a removable hardtop. He was ecstatic with joy; he finally was able to buy something he really liked. He would take Clara and me for rides everywhere in his beautiful car, and we were just happy to be driving around with him.

While he worked at the electronic company, he worked on a piece of electronic machinery that would simulate the sounds of a submarine. This test equipment would be used in Navy vessels. It would track other ships with its sonar gear, and it was used to calibrate the sonar gear. The test could simulate sounds that were able to locate where the boat was coming from.

Goddard Space Flight Center

Vince applied for a job with NASA at Goddard Space Center, and because he had experience at the electronics company, they hired him. While he worked at Goddard, he continued his education by attending night school at Johns Hopkins.

Vince met a wonderful lady while he worked at Goddard. Her name was Grace. She was very special to him because they were both interested in the same things, science and outer space. After they dated for some time, they decided to get married. They picked the famous Wye Oak Tree in Maryland to have their marriage ceremony on August 23, 1975. As we did many times in the past, we went to Sabatino's to celebrate Vince's wedding to Grace with a delicious dinner which consisted of their tender Veal Francese and their homemade Gnocchi with their fresh Marinara sauce, and salad with their outstanding house dressing. They have had a wonderful life together, and produced one child. Her name is Andrea, and she is a beautiful and intelligent young lady today.

While working at Goddard, Vince built a film recorder that would process data of scenes over the earth into images. Before this recorder was developed, the procedure took a long time. The electronics that Vince designed turned the pictures into a quick-look film recorder that took only twenty-five seconds per image.

The Discovery on Mars

While he was working at NASA, he heard about the discovery of a face on Mars. He performed his own research with data from the planet Mars, because of his unique knowledge of image processing and computers. He went to the archives at NASA at the National Space Science Data Center in building 26 and asked for the original data tapes of the face. After asking for permission for use of the film recorder during off-hours, he then reprocessed the image through the film recorder. After confirming that the face was a real structure, he published a lengthy book describing all of the information he had collected through the years, including fossils in meteorites from Mars. Now they have acknowledged that there were oceans of water on Mars, when all along Vince was saying the same thing twenty-five years ago.

After this publication, he was asked to go on many speaking tours. On one of his speaking tours at the Massachusetts Institute of Technology, they told him he had done such terrific research, that he should have earned a Ph.D. He even went on a speaking tour in Berlin, Germany, about the face on Mars. Vince also addressed the members and guests of the Engineering Colloquia at the Goddard Space Center on his findings and images from Mars. After he did all of this research, some other people started to copy his work, to make it appear they were the ones who found the face on Mars. These people gave my brother a lot of aggravation. He did not want any confrontation from them, so he just stopped fighting them, and continued to work at Goddard for twenty-five years.

I was upset because despite of Vince's talent and hard work he never received the recognition that he deserved. Regardless of this, we are all aware of his intelligence, and we are all very proud of him.

Vincent DiPietro in Glen Burnie,
Maryland, June 1970.

Eleven: High School Graduation

It was my senior year in High School and I tried out for the senior play. To my surprise, I was selected for the part of the crazy maid. The play was called *The Bat*. Despite the fact that it was supposed to be a mystery, it turned out to be more of a comedy. I was the maid, and in one part of the show, I had to run around on the stage in my night clothes with my hair up in curlers screaming, "He's after me, he's after me." The audience was in stitches. We had practiced long and hard hours to make the show a hit. The audience loved it. They gave us several curtain calls. We had to wear heavy make-up, because the teacher said this would help the people in the audience to see our facial expressions. It took forever to get the make-up off my face, and I wondered how movie stars could wear all this thick make-up. Mom, Dad, Vince, and Rose attended the play, and Vince, who had become an expert photographer, took pictures of me on stage. I had so much fun doing the show. There were all kind of parties after the show, and for a little while I was a star, and it was nice.

Naturally, my parents had to have a party to celebrate my accomplishments in the play. We all had another great time laughing, eating, and drinking at Mom and Dad's. As graduation approached, I was sorry I did not enroll in the academic courses, because I realized if I went to college, I could pursue acting, something I wanted to do all of my life. One of my regrets in life was not having a chance to further my education. I know now I could have still attended college, but by the time I realized this, I did not have the resources.

The Senior Prom

It was getting close to my senior prom and I met a boy through Clara. He was Italian, tall, and so handsome with a mustache. His father was the local undertaker; and he came from a good family that my parents knew. There use to be dances at churches in the neighborhood Clara and I would attend, as did all the kids who went to Pompei and St. Leo's. On Friday night, we would go to the dance at St. Leo's, Saturday night we would go to another dance at Our Lady of Fatima, and Sunday the dance was always at Pompei's. This is where I met this gorgeous boy. He was also a fantastic dancer, something that we both loved to do. This is how we became connected. I finally got up enough courage to ask him to go to my senior prom with me, and to my surprise, he said yes. I was on cloud nine.

I had a job after school at Woolworth's five and dime store on Eastern Avenue. I made fifteen dollars a week, (a big deal back then), most of which I gave to Dad. Into the five and dime store walked this handsome guy, while I was working, and he wanted to know what color my dress was so he could buy me flowers to wear at the prom. I was living in a fantasy world, because I was under the impression that he really cared for me. Mom and I went to purchase the prom dress. Etta's and Becky's were stores on Broadway that sold the prettiest prom dresses ever, so Mom and I took the bus there to buy the dress. Oh, how beautiful the dress was, red and full, and right in Mom's price range.

The big night of the prom finally arrived. I had my hair done, and I really looked extraordinary. The boy pulled up in front of my house in his father's big black limousine that they used for funerals, and after taking many pictures, and all of the neighbors looking out their doors to see who was going in the big limousine, off to the prom we went. I felt like I was living a dream come true. I just knew it would be a fantastic evening. I had a pretty good time at the prom, because all of my classmates were there. But through the course of the evening, the boy kept leaving me. He would take off, and I could not find him for some time. I did not worry about this though because I was having fun with my friends.

After the prom, everyone decided to go to Little Italy to eat because there was a restaurant that stayed opened until late called Sabatino's.

While we were in the restaurant eating, someone decided to go to some person's shore home and continue the party. I was having a great time, so I thought we would all leave the restaurant for the shore party. When we got to the shore home, every one paired off, and oh yes, the boy wanted me to have sex with him. I really did not know how to do anything; I was still a virgin. I thought he liked me, I really thought he liked me, but I soon found out what he was really after. When I refused him, the boy left me; he just got up and left me there all alone. I really did not know the other couples that well so I just stayed there outside all alone until the light of the morning came and I asked someone to take me home. I was heartbroken. I really liked this guy, and he left me there all alone, something that I would become used to all of my life. When I arrived home, Mom covered for me, especially when I told her what happened to me; she felt sorry for me. This was the end of my big night at the prom. What a disappointment.

Graduation Day

Graduation day was here, and because of all the different activities that were going on then it was a very thrilling time for me. I had to get my graduation gown, buy a dress for the occasion, and get tickets to accommodate as many family members as possible for the graduation ceremony. I had to practice marching down the aisle with my classmates singing our class song, "The Battle Hymn of the Republic." What a beautiful song it was.

As the day finally came, and everyone was dressed in our caps and gowns, we marched down the aisle all starry-eyed. We were called up to the stage to receive our diploma, from our principal Mr. Woelper. There was not a dry eye in the place as we sang our class song. We were all crying, because we knew we would not be seeing each other that much anymore as we would all be going our separate ways. Our whole future was before us now, because we had many things to look forward to. We would also miss going to school. I loved my years in high school because of all the different activities that I was involved in. For us attending school was more a joy than a chore.

After the ceremony was over, the family headed over to my house for the big party. My aunts and uncles were there, and there was plenty of food and drink for all to enjoy again.

Dad had to work that day, and when he came home, he had a black eye. There was a guy at work who was jealous of him, because

Dad was a hard working man and was just trying to do his job. This man confronted dad after work and started to pick a fight with him. Dad had to fight this man off. He had to defend himself. Dad said, "Oh, yes, I have a black eye, but you should see the other guy." Dad was so strong. Vince bought a moving picture camera, he became the photographer for the whole family, and everyone wanted to be in the moving pictures. He took pictures of Dad and me walking through the rose garden and took pictures of everyone eating around the kitchen table. Mom and Dad planned this beautiful affair for me to celebrate my graduation.

After graduation, I began working in an office that was not far from my house. The job consisted of typing invoices to people who owed money to the company. It was boring, but it was the first real paying job, and I loved it because I was able to buy things for myself (clothes in sizes three and five, and shoes). Wow, it was wonderful shopping with my own money, buying my own things.

Home Alone

In the summer, Mom, Dad, and Rosie went to the ocean for a week's vacation. Vince was now in the Army. I was working, and I could not go away with my parents. Johnny had gotten a job at Gino's restaurant, which had just opened and was not far from our house. Johnny worked the night shift, but I did not realize the place stayed open so late in the evening.

When Mom and Dad went away for their vacation, I thought, "Oh boy, I am going to have a great time staying up late with my friends," but my friends could not get permission to stay up late with me. Their parents were home, so they all had to be home early. That left me home alone on the couch, waiting for Johnny to come home. I was afraid of being in the old and creepy house all alone. There were noises coming from everywhere. I was afraid to go upstairs and sleep in my room, so I just stayed on the couch waiting for Johnny. Mom had French provincial furniture, which is not comfortable enough to sleep on.

When Johnny finally came home, I said, "Where have you been?"

"Working," he said, "I had to take the bus home." I was glad to have him home I hugged and kissed him, and then we both finally went upstairs to go to sleep.

Aunt Lena and Aunt Jenny worried about Johnny and me being home alone and not having any food to eat. Being the Italian women that they were, my two Aunts had to make sure that we would not starve until Mom and Dad came home. They both brought food over to the house so we would not go hungry. They always cared about our well-being. You might have thought our parents were going to be away for a long period of time instead of just a week. With all of these protectors around me, you would never think anything bad could happen to me.

The Two Father Lou's

Even the two Father Lou's, the priests from church, checked on us to make sure we were okay. The two Father Lou's had become such good friends they would always be teasing each other when they made their sermons on the pulpit on Sunday. They called Father Lou Esposito "Father Lou #1" (he was the Priest stationed at Pompei Church), and Father Lou Trotta "Father Lou #2" (he was stationed in New York). "Father Lou number two" would come home to Baltimore for a visit during the summer, Christmas, and Easter holidays, because his whole family still lived here, and this is how the two Father Lou's became the best of friends.

The people from the neighborhood and the priests from Pompei all said that "Father Lou number two" would never make it as a priest. Well, he has been a priest for fifty-five years. Father Lou Trotta was considered the original "Peck's bad boy" of the neighborhood, and this is why everyone said he would never make it as a priest. He was always getting in fights and causing a lot of hardship for his family.

"Father Lou number one" was very kind and gentle and all the little children followed him all around. They loved him so and wanted to always be in his presence. He was the first young priest to come to Our Lady of Pompei, and he was someone to whom the children could relate. The two priests would go to Patterson Park and play tennis together. When the children found out that the two Father Lou's were going to Patterson Park to play tennis, they followed the priests there. Sometimes the children would play tennis with them. The children loved to see them kidding and teasing one another, because it was like a big comedy show. This would keep the children engaged, and in doing this, the priests would bring the children close to God and the church.

A star is born: Peachy in the school play *The Bat* at
Patterson High, June 1959.

Twelve: Living the Good Life

Clara and I had been the best of friends since we were young. We went everywhere together. She knew all the best places to go to dance or to just go and have lots of fun.

There was a store on Eastern Avenue called the Arundel where all of the young people in Highlandtown would meet. It was a great place to hang out and grab a soda. In those days, there were no drugs, no fighting, and no shootings, just a nice place to go and meet friends and find out where the big dance would be on Saturday night.

We had a special friend from Pompei School named Joe, who would also be at the soda shop. Joe had a car, and he would take us for rides everywhere. We would all pitch in for gas, but of course, the gas prices were not what they are today. We would all throw in a quarter apiece to fill the tank up and then go for our ride. A donut shop had just opened up in Essex, and we had never seen anything like it before, so naturally we had to go and check it out. Joe would take us for a ride there all the time, because this was the latest craze, and we could not get enough of it. I think we all gained a few pounds then, but it did not matter, because we danced off those pounds every Saturday night.

Ameche's Drive In

There was also a drive-in hamburger shop called Ameche's which opened up on Loch Raven Boulevard. Allan Ameche and Johnny Unitas were two of the most famous Baltimore Colts football players. The Colts won the NFL championship in 1958 and '59, and Ameche's was the most popular place for young people to go.

Vince liked taking Clara and me for rides in his new Thunderbird. Clara found out about Ameche's, and she asked Vince if he would take us for a ride to check out the new place. It was such a neat place; you could pull up to a speaker and order your food. Then a girl would bring your food out to you. She would hook the tray up to the car window, so you could eat the food right in your car. We just thought this was the greatest idea.

Goin' Downy Oshun, Hon

During the summer, Clara wanted me to go to Ocean City with her. It was, and still is, the place where all the kids go during the summer. I had to get this "okayed" by you-know-who first: Mom and Dad. How was I ever going to get past Dad so I could go to the ocean for the weekend? Dear sweet Mom came through at the last minute. I do not know how she managed this one, but I was allowed to go down the ocean.

Before we went to the ocean, I bought a pair of contact lenses for myself, because I was almost blind in my right eye. Years ago, when Dad took me to the eye doctor, the doctor told Dad he did not know how I was ever able to see because the vision in my right eye was so terrible. This was the reason I had such a problem in school.

The teacher used to put the test on the blackboard back when I was in school. I could not see, and every time I asked to be put up front, by the time I got there, the tests were over.

None of the nuns knew my eyesight was this bad. They thought I was just fooling when I asked to be moved up front. I had been wearing glasses ever since the fourth grade and I hated them. I wanted to get contact lenses for such a long time, and when I finally got the opportunity to do so, my self-esteem improved considerably.

Finally, the weekend arrived, and Clara and I went to the ocean, and had a great time. Almost everyone from school and the neighborhood was there. We rented a room that was all the way at the end of the boardwalk, where the rates were cheap. It was a dive, but it was in our price range, so we did not care what it looked like. We had no other choice, although when we arrived at our room we found out the place was full of ants, we could not wait to get out of there. We could not afford to move, so we spent all of our days on the beach, and all of our nights walking the boardwalk to avoid the ants. We would sleep on the beach during the day so we could stay up all night. I wore my hair in a huge beehive, the style then. Everyone could see my hair coming before they saw me. I always dressed stylish and kept myself neat.

Staying "down the ocean" was a big treat for me. It was my first time away from my parents, and I felt grown up. Since I had just got my contact lenses, I spent my whole time worrying I might lose them. They felt as though they were going to fall out of my eyes. I walked around all day holding my head up high. I did not even go in the water because I thought that I might lose my contact lenses. The old contact lenses moved all around in your eyes until they formed a groove in your eye. This is why they felt like they were going to fall out.

After a weekend at the ocean, I came home and continued to work during the week and go out with Clara on the weekends. Even though she became a hairdresser, and I worked in an office, we managed to get together on the weekends so we could go dancing. I became such a terrific dancer, and guys were constantly asking me to jitterbug with them. While we were dancing, people would clap their hands and form a circle around us. Other people took turns dancing, and everyone stood around clapping. Clara and I always had a good time dancing on the weekend.

Having Fun

Clara and I continued going to the ocean on holiday weekends like Memorial Day, the 4th of July, and Labor Day. There would always be a bunch of girls sharing a room, so we could afford to go to the ocean a lot. One time, there was a huge riot in Ocean City.

There were no big hotels on the beach like there are now. The boardwalk stopped at 9th street. Just past 9th street, this part of the beach was called the dunes. There would just be mounds and mounds of sand everywhere. It was easy to have parties there because you could hide behind the large piles of sand. There would be one party over there and a clambake over here and so on and so on.

We were just having some fun. However, when the cops found out what the kids were doing and that some kids brought beer they came down to break up the party. No one was allowed to stay on the beach after dark. The kids got upset, and many of them rebelled. The cops came out in full force. When Clara and I found out the cops were coming, we left in a hurry.

A lot of kids were locked up, but we were lucky enough to get away. None of the kids we knew from Highlandtown were arrested. Clara and I were both lucky to get away before the cops came. We stayed at the lower part of the boardwalk, away from all the action, because we did not want to be arrested. There were places that stayed open all night long, and we would go there and stay and have coffee all night. I knew if I got in trouble, I would still have to answer to a higher power—Dad. I knew the consequences at home would be a lot worse than spending a night in jail.

The kids were upset that the cops had broken up their fun and this is the reason why the kids started to revolt. Later that evening, the cops came up to the lower end of the boardwalk and began to lock up some more kids. The only way the cops could break up the crowds was to turn the hoses on them. As the kids tried to run away, they were hosed down, and then they were caught and were locked up. It was a huge mess.

The Road Home from OC

On one unforgettable occasion, when Clara's boyfriend was driving all of us home from Ocean City, I was always the back seat driver and everyone would tell me to be quiet. They said I was overly cautious. On this particular trip as we were coming home, a car in front of us was crossing the median strip very slowly. In fact, it was creeping along. We were just coming out of Ocean City and were on Route 50, and we were traveling a little fast.

I was going to say, "watch out for the car up ahead," but I did not want them to tell me to be quiet again, so I just did not say anything. Clara's boyfriend did not slow down, and we were getting closer and closer to the car that was crossing the median. I do not know what Clara's boyfriend was thinking, but he just never slowed down. Before I knew what happened, we broadsided the car. Our car turned all around, and smoke filled the air. Both cars landed on the other side of the road. All this happened before seat belts, but I know that God had to be with us because no one was seriously injured. The only thing that happened was that we got some scrapes and bruises.

We had to hitch a ride home because the car was demolished. Just then, my friend from school, Joe, who used to take us riding around town, came driving down the road. He was on his way home and saw us on the side of the road, so he stopped to see if he could help us. The only big issue was that we all had lots of luggage. Down the road came another one of Joe's friends, who also pulled over to see if he could help. We were so fortunate that we had such good friends to bring us and our luggage home. We were all grateful that no one got seriously hurt.

Peachy at Bayshore Beach with brothers Steve "Buckwheat" Cerra and Mike Cerra, July 1960. The Cerra family lived on Pratt Street and owned a store at Pratt and Conkling Streets.

Thirteen: Broken Dreams

I found a new job at a collection agency in downtown Baltimore. It took a long time to get there because the bus was a cross-country bus and the route that it took went round about the city. I would have to get up extra early so I would not be late. The job was more interesting than my first one because my boss would send me to different companies that hired our company to collect money for them. I had to go through their files and send letters to the people who owed money. The letters stated that if they did not pay, we would take them to debtor's court. It was not monotonous, and I got to meet new people.

Mr. Ellis, who was my boss, also sent me to restaurants in the neighborhood to buy his lunch. He was Jewish and ate different kinds of food that were unfamiliar to me. I only ate Italian and American dishes, but pickin up his lunch exposed me to all sort of new delicious food.

There was a girl who I worked with, and we became friends. She had a boyfriend who did not treat her well, but she told me she loved him anyway. No matter what I said to try to change her mind, it would not matter. She would not pay any attention to me because she loved him. She told me about her boyfriend's friend who had a car and asked me if we could go on a double date sometime. I said okay because I did not think that anything would be wrong with this. I was a very trusting person.

The Deceitful Employee

Once a week, we would have to work late to get the invoices out on time. On this one night, Mr. Ellis came in extremely upset. He asked the bookkeeper to come into his office. We were all nervous because no one knew what was going on. We found out later that the bookkeeper had embezzled money from the company. This man was well liked by everyone in the office and it shocked us to find out what he had done. How could he do this to our wonderful boss, who treated everyone equally? I would never do anything like this. Mom and Dad taught all of us to be honest and respect our elders. This was driven into our heads just about every day of our lives. "Be honest and respect your elders," Dad would say over and over again. Dad also taught me to keep my eyes and ears open and my mouth closed. He told me, "You can learn a lot this way." It was another one of Dad's great proverbs. The embezzler was prosecuted and then sent to jail.

Broken Heart

When I went out on the weekends with Clara, I met this fantastic guy named John. He was a fabulous dancer and we became inseparable. Our courtship started out as just dancing partners, and it developed into a full-blown relationship. John would take me to all the hot spots to go dancing, and I was under the impression that he really cared about me. However, as the relationship moved along, he wanted more from me than just kisses and petting.

I would not give into him because I was brought up to be a good Catholic girl. All of a sudden, he stopped calling me, as though we had nothing together. I was heartbroken. It was my first real relationship, and John just left me with no explanation at all.

That weekend Clara told me to go out with her. She said, "Come on, Peach, you can't stay in all weekend and cry over him. You have to go out. It will make you feel better, come on." So out we went, and to my surprise there was John on the dance floor with a beautiful blonde. I was crushed.

I wanted to run away and cry my eyes out, but Clara made me stay with her, acting as if I was having a good time. She wanted me to act like it did not bother me that John was with another girl. What was wrong with me? When was I ever going to be able to change my way of thinking? I had to realize that if I did not give in to guys, I was not going to be able to keep one. Broken hearted and let down again, I didn't understand how he could begin a relationship with someone new this week when we had just been together last week. And then

I realized that he must have been seeing this girl the whole time he was seeing me.

I had to keep going on with my life. I could not dwell on this forever. I had cried enough, and now I was going to move on. I kept pondering the idea of what my friend from work had talked to me about going out with her boyfriend's friend. I made up my mind that when my friend from work asked me to go on a double date again, I would go.

The Boy, the Rape, the Baby

So one time when the girl from work asked me to go on a double date, I said "yes." Whenever I went out with a boy, he was someone I had known for some time, but here I was, going out on a blind date for the first time. The three of them came to my house to pick me up. We were supposed to go to the movies, but instead we went to a drive-in theater, another thing that I had never done before.

My blind date Mike Dixon was kind of cute. His flamboyant style suggested that he thought he was better than anyone else; he was always showing off about his clothes and car. He talked with a New York accent, even though he was not from New York. Being the naive person, I thought everything was going to be okay. As soon as we got to the drive-in theater, Mike started to paw all over me. I had to fight him off all night long. My friend and her boyfriend were in the back seat making out and not paying any attention to me, even though I was struggling in the front seat fighting Mike off during the whole movie.

Finally, the movie was over, and Mike took our friends home first. I thought he was going to take me on home, but instead he drove to a secluded spot somehwere and attacked me. He told me if I did not give in to him that he would shoot me. I did not know what to do. I had never been in a situation like this before. I was with a guy I did not know at all in an unfamiliar part of town. I could not believe anyone could be so cruel. Sadly, I could not fight him off and before I knew it, he pinned me down and raped me.

After he finally stopped, he took me home and told me not to say a word or he would hurt me. I was in shock and did not know what to do. I did not know where Mike lived or what he did, so how could I do anything anyway? All kinds of thoughts went through my head. What would Dad do to me if he found out? What would he do to this guy if he ever found him? What if I got pregnant? Oh my God, what was I going to do?

I was ashamed of what had happened to me, and I was too young and inexperienced to realize it was not my fault. I did not want to tell anyone. I could not go to Clara because I was too ashamed. Since I believed it was my fault, I just kept quiet.

When Mike called me to go out with him again, it was as if he had powers over me. He acted as if I owed him something. He did not even mention what he had done to me. He treated me like spoiled material. He made me feel as if no one else would want to go out with me now. I was never frightened of anyone the way I was frightened of him.

I thought, "What if I'm pregnant?" What would I do then? What would I tell my parents? To whom could I talk? Finally, I confided in Mike because I thought I might be pregnant and I had nowhere else to turn. His attitude toward me changed and he started treating me nicely. I do not know why, maybe he was afraid of what my parents would do to him if I were pregnant.

Still Mike made me feel like I had done something wrong, and I had to do whatever he said. In those days, if anything like this happened, and a girl got pregnant, it was considered the girl's fault. People would say that the girls led the boys on. It was a bad time for women then; men were everything, and women were supposed to be home doing housework. I was living in the "Ozzie and Harriet" era. Mom and Dad had kept me so sheltered from the outside world that I was never prepared for anything like this. I did not know what to do, so I continued to keep quiet.

When it came time for my period, it never came. Then my nerves got the best of me. I was so upset, and because of the way I was acting, Mom had a feeling that there was something wrong. She always said that she was a psychic because she was born on January 6th, the day three wise men visited the baby Jesus. She would always say she had special powers.

She called Aunt Lena, and both of them took me upstairs to

Mom's bedroom and started to question me. I told them what had happened to me, but I left out the gruesome details, especially the one about being threatened. Aunt Lena told me that if I was pregnant, I could get an abortion and she would help pay for some of the expenses. She had a big heart. They wanted me to go to the doctor to find out if I was pregnant. Nobody would talk about anything like this back then because everything was "hush-hush" in those days.

I did not know Mike had told his mother and his sister that I might be pregnant. The two of them started calling Mom on the phone every day. They were filling her head with a bunch of lies about me. They told Mom that Mike was engaged to a nice girl, and I was luring him away from her. Mom was so sweet; she had never been associated with such deceitful people before, but she defended me. I never found out about how they tormented Mom every day until much later.

What I had expected came true. I was pregnant. Being Catholic, I never considered the proposition Aunt Lena suggested. There would not be an abortion. When I told Mike that I was pregnant, he said we could run away and get married. For a little while, he became a different person. He was actually nice to me. Maybe his mother and sister were giving him a hard time.

Still bewildered, I agreed to marry Mike. We went to get a marriage license, but little did I know they reported all licenses in the newspaper. Mom's nosy neighbor saw it and questioned her. By now, I was determined to go through with the marriage to Mike. I thought this was the right thing to do, that all I had to do was get married and everything would be all right. After all, didn't Mom and Dad have a great marriage? I was living in a fantasy world. I believed that I could have a great marriage also.

The Marriage

We planned to be married somewhere in Anne Arundel County just south of Baltimore City. Mike said that he knew a church in Brooklyn where we could get married with no questions asked. I wanted to go to a church where no one knew us. Finally, on a cold and nasty Sunday afternoon, as a mix of rain and snow fell, we began our new life together.

Mike never knew the exact location of the church, so inevitably we wound up at the wrong church somewhere in Brooklyn. The minister had activities going on that day at the church, but I believe he felt sorry for us when he saw that we had come in such inclement weather. He performed a quick marriage service right in his office. It left me with such a cold feeling, nothing at all as I had imagined my wedding would be like. And it set the stage for my entire married life to Mike, just one big disaster after another. I had been to so many family weddings. All my cousins got married in a Catholic church, and everything was beautiful with flowers everywhere and music playing. A Catholic priest performed those ceremonies and everything was perfect. The church was always full of relatives and there would be a big party afterwards. It was exactly the opposite of my wedding. None of that happened for me.

I was upset, but I just kept thinking that I was doing the right thing and everything would work out. You know, when you are young, you are full of great expectations. I thought I could overcome all obstacles. I thought that with the baby coming, everything would be okay. I kept thinking of the great marriage my parents had, and I thought I would have a marriage like they did.

The Pregnancy

When Mom found out that we had gotten married and I was pregnant, she bought me some things so Mike and I could move into an apartment together. She bought me a few nightgowns, and what a strange trousseau it was: flannel nightgowns that came up to my neck, down to my wrists, and down to my feet. Very sexy! I guess she was still trying to protect me. She knew how cold I always was at night.

Our first apartment was down the street from Aunt Lena, on the second floor above of a beauty shop. The apartment was full of roaches. I did not even know what roaches were. What were these ugly bugs that were everywhere? I tried to make a nice dinner for Mike for our first night at the apartment. I wanted him to have something to eat when he came home from working in the barbershop late at night. I was trying to make some kind of a life for us.

However, the first dinner I made was almost attacked by roaches. I sat in the middle of the living room on the coffee table holding the dinner in my arms so the roaches would not get in it. Needless to say, we moved out that night.

After this, Mike moved me all the way over to Brooklyn, a part of town that I was not familiar with, and it was also far away from Highlandtown. I had to take two buses to get to work every day. If that was not bad enough, it was so far off the bus line, I had a long hike coming and going to the apartment.

Our landlords treated us wonderfully though, and the apartment was spotless. Then the morning sickness came. Oh, how I dreaded it. I tried everything, but I could not stop being sick. I threw up every morning for three months straight.

I worked at the office downtown until the month that my baby was to be born. When I worked for the collection agency in the '60s, computers were just starting to become popular. My boss had someone come in and show all of us how to operate the computer. Had I stayed at this job, I would have become a computer whiz by now. I worked up until a couple weeks before I was supposed to give birth. We decided to stay at Mike's brother's place in the country for a while. We had to go all the way down a bumpy road to get to their shore home. The roads were not as developed as they are today, because most of the houses in Lake Shore were considered summer homes. Out of Mike's whole family, Pat and Pouche (who was Mike's brother) were the only two people who treated me as if I was a good person. Their house was small, and they had a couple of children, but they made room for us to stay with them.

When I was at Pat and Pouche's house, their little boy was out playing one day when all of a sudden he came to the front door with a bucket full of crickets. He wanted to bring them in the house to show them to his mother. Being the city girl that I was, I put my foot up to the front door, and called for his mother. "Pat," I yelled, "come and see what your son wants to bring into the house."

Pat had such a diplomatic way about her; she could handle any situation. She said to her son, "You can't bring crickets into the house; they need to live outside because that's where their house is." I really loved her, because she treated me like I was a normal person.

My First Child

Our stay at the shore home was cut short because all the long rides on the bumpy roads must have disturbed something with the baby and by Sunday morning it was ready to be born. I called Mercy Hospital in Baltimore and was told to wait until the contractions got closer. I told them I was far away from the hospital, and I was afraid to wait any longer. If something happened, it would take us a long time to get to the hospital. So Mike and I decided to head to the hospital in Baltimore. However, by the time we arrived, there were no more pains. I was in the hospital all day, and the nurses left me in a room with lots of screaming women. I thought to myself, "Wow, this is going to be horrible; when are the pains going to start?"

But the pains did not come and I became frightened because the nurses left me alone for such a long time. Finally, I was allowed to go out in the waiting room to visit with my parents and Mike. I stayed with them for a long time, for I did not want to go back in the room with all of those crying women.

After hours of waiting and wondering what was going to happen, the pains started to come fast and furious. Following a long ordeal of pushing and bearing down, my beautiful baby was born at 9:10 P.M. on September 16, 1962. I decided to name her Anna Maria—Anna after my grandmother Annarella and Maria because the show "West Side Story" had just opened. There was such a beautiful song called "Maria," and she was the main character in the play. I just loved that song.

Anna Maria was lovely and her head was covered with beautiful black hair. I just could not believe this gorgeous creature had come from me. After we brought her home from the hospital, and whenever we took her anywhere, people would look at her and ask if she was a real baby. She was perfect in every way; she looked just like a little baby doll.

Left: Peachy and Mike outside 3510 Claremont Street, April 1962.
Right: Peachy, Mike, and baby Anna Maria, May 1962.

Fourteen: The Abuse

On October 20, 1962, a little while after Anna was born, Vincent got married. The whole family attended. Mom and Dad were dressed so beautifully. Johnny was the best man, little Rosie was the flower girl. All of the aunts, uncles, and cousins were there. It was a lovely affair. Everyone was having a great time; everyone but me. All the things that happened to me just hit me all at once. This was the kind of wedding I had always dreamed of, and now it would never happen. I just started to cry. It was a good thing that I was sitting in the back of the church so that my parents could not see me. I just lost my composure. If it were not for my cousin Freddie coming over to console me, I would not have been able to control myself. I did not want to spoil my brother's wedding. I did not want Mom and Dad to see me this way. Freddie stayed with me until I was able to calm down. I went to the reception as if everything was all right. I did not want to spoil Vince's wedding.

After spending the day with my family, I went home to pick up Anna and hugged and kissed her because it was the first time I had left her since she was born. She was such a blessing to me. Mike could not go to the wedding because it was on a Saturday, which was his busiest day at the barbershop. When Mike came home from work, we played with the baby and just had a good time being together for this evening. Mike brought home a Monopoly game and we would play it for hours. Of course, he would cheat like crazy. In fact, we both did, this was the only way that you could get control of any property and for a while, everything was fine.

After I married Mike, and started living with him, I found out that he took strange pills often when his friends were around. They would come over to the apartment, hang out for a bit, then go play pinball machines somewhere all night long. Much later I concluded that those pills must have been uppers of some kind since they kept the guys up all night, but at the time I did not question it.

Eventually, Mike's friends came around more often, they took more pills together, and they stayed out all night every weekend. He told me not to make a big deal about it, and he assured me that he would never take heroin (like some of his friends did). He said he could never put a needle in his arm. He always took pills, as most of his friends did, and I was under the impression that this is what he was still doing. He stayed out all night and came home in the wee small hours of the morning. I tried to ignore this and kept trying to make a go of our marriage. I kept the apartment clean and had dinner ready when Mike came home from work, but nothing mattered to him. He would come home every night during the week, but when it came to Saturday (his payday), he would stay out until Sunday evening, spending all of his pay, and leaving me and Anna home alone all weekend. I knew about the pills, but I did not know that they could control your whole life. I was young and naive, I did not know anything about the drugs or the affect that they could have on you, but when he was coming down from the pills, he would become nasty.

When I questioned him about where he had been, he would say, "Leave me alone," and if I pursued the issue, he would beat me. This is when the worst part of the abuse started. I received many beatings when I questioned him about where he had been, or told him that I needed money to buy food for the baby. I would have to avoid Mom and Dad so they would not see the bruises. I did not want to hurt them any more than I already had.

I think Mike moved me to Brooklyn because he knew I would be far away from my parents. And since we did not have a phone, I could not get in touch with them. The apartment that we now lived in belonged to his aunt, so if he missed a rent payment, he would not have to worry that she would evict us. I am sure that his mother stepped in and talked to her sister asking her to let us stay there.

Mike was getting more and more into his habit and more and more into his friends and further and further away from me and Anna. We barely had food to eat, but I always made sure he would buy food for the baby. He was a barber and made tips during the week, and I would make him take me to the store to buy food for Anna. I always had bread and milk, so I would make mayonnaise and mustard sandwiches for myself, and when I added salt and pepper they were not that bad.

The situation was getting progressively worse. Whenever we had a fight, and I tried to defend myself, he would turn into a maniac. One time, I hit him back, and he punched me in the face, knocking me clear across the room. After this, I never tried to hit him again. I just took the beatings, repeatedly accepting my fate. Eventually I would stop questioning his actions because I wanted to avoid the beatings. I tried to leave him many times, but he would always beg me to stay. He would tell me he was going to change, but he never did. I was far away from my parents, and I did not want to burden them with my hard times. I did not want my parents to see me with my black eyes or my battered and bruised body. Dad would always say, "What is going to happen to Leonora if anything happens to me?" He was still around and I was already falling apart.

Trying to Elude Mike

Once when I asked Mike where he was going he beat me very bad. I just wanted to get away so he could not find me. I had a black eye and a large bruise on my forehead from the brutality and Mike left me again to fix my wounds. After this, I called dear sweet Aunt Jenny and asked her if I could come and stay with her for a while, and she told me I could stay at her house. I was worried for little Anna. I had to get away from him. I just wanted to scare him to make him think I had left him for good. I thought this would make a difference to him if he could not find me.

I guess Mike must have called my parents' house, and I am sure Aunt Jenny called Mom also, because soon everyone was calling my aunt's house and wanting to know what I was going to do. I just wanted to shock Mike into thinking I had left him and meant it this time. Every time I tried to do something, it never turned out the way I planned.

In the meantime, I got everyone involved in my troubles. I had a decision to make and I was so confused. I was so bewildered and very young and still presuming everything would be okay if I went back with him. By this time, both of my brothers were ready to punch Mike's lights out. Later I found out that Dad wanted to have him "taken care of." The one thing I did not want to occur had happened. I got everyone involved in my dilemma. Mike kept calling me and crying to me and telling me how much he loved me and how much he missed me and wanted me back, and—foolish, foolish me—I returned to him. Things were okay for a while until the same pattern started all over again because he couldn't stay away from his narcotics. Needless to say, I made the wrong decision again and I got everyone upset when I went back to Mike.

The Death of a President

When the beatings started yet again, I left Mike and moved back with my parents. I got a job working at a company that was not far from where I was living. It did not pay much, but I had some money to buy the things I needed. I had worked there for a while when all of a sudden one day something terrible happened. The news came into the office, "President Kennedy has been shot!" Everything stopped in the office. We all had our ears glued to the radio. How could this have happened? What a great president he was. I can remember watching his press conferences when I was in the apartment. He had great responses for all the questions that the press asked of him. His answers were witty, and everyone loved him. He knew how to work the press, and by the time the press conference was over, he would have them all agreeing with him.

He had the most beautiful wife, and I tried to copy her style, as did everyone else. While they were in the White House, they would be referred to living their lives as if they were in Camelot. They were a young couple and they had two lovely children. The public could not get enough of them. They were treated like royalty. I just thought they were wonderful, and so did the whole nation. How could anyone do this horrible thing to such a wonderful man, my President? How could you not feel compassion for the way President Kennedy died and all the events that followed? The whole country was in mourning. Reporters broke down and cried when they spoke about him on TV.

For days, America was in shock. We were all mesmerized because there were so many details that kept unfolding right in front of our eyes on our TV sets. I can remember being with the family in front of the TV watching everything at Aunt Lena's house on Sunday when we saw the whole story unfold. Uncle Mimi was at Aunt Lena's also and he could not understand how someone could do this horrible thing. I never paid much attention to politics (because of all the drama that was happening in my life), but after this awful thing happened to President Kennedy, I started to pay more attention to what was going on in politics. I could not get enough of it then.

More Abuse

Mike started to come around again, telling me how much he missed Anna and me and crying to me again and telling me how much he loved me. He promised that he would never ever hurt me again. Still being the naive person that I was, I believed him. I would meet him away from my parents' home, for I truly believed he cared for me. I was living in a dream world, and I wanted to have a life just like Mom and Dad. I wanted to have someone love me the way Dad loved Mom. I kept wishing this would happen for me, but it never did. I had no idea he just wanted to lure me back to him so he would have a place to stay. He had aggravated his family so much they did not want anything to do with him. Foolishly, I took him back again hoping for a world like Doris Day and Rock Hudson had in the movies. I watched so many movies that I believed real life could be like this make-believe world, but the one thing Doris Day did not have in those films was a drug-addict husband.

After taking Mike back this time, we got along all right for a while again. We moved to a nice apartment, and he even took me on a vacation to Atlantic City. I had not been on a vacation with him, or anywhere nice for that matter, ever. I was happy to go but sad that I had to leave Anna behind with my parents. While we were on the road to Atlantic City, he told me his friends were going to meet us there also.

Needless to say, we did not have a good time while we were in Atlantic City. Every time we went anywhere, his friends were always there with us. They had to be involved in everything that Mike did.

He could not stand being without them either. I became irritated about the whole situation. I just wanted to go home.

I said, "Why did you take me all the way to Atlantic City if you had no intention of spending time with me? I could have stayed home with Anna, and you could have been with your friends in Baltimore. Why did we come here? I thought we were going to be alone." I walked away from him, and started to walk alone on the boardwalk crying and wondering what I should do, and what a mess I had made of my life by believing his lies.

All of a sudden, Mike was in front of me. I do not understand how he found me, I mean you know how big Atlantic City is, and he found me walking on the boardwalk. After this attempt at a romantic gesture, his friends left Atlantic City and we finally had some sort of time alone together. It really did not matter though because it was clear he did not want to be with me. He wanted to be with his friends so he could take his drugs.

When we came back from Atlantic City, Mike told me to quit my job, that he would take care of me, and again I believed him. It did not last long though and some weeks later he was back to his old routine. After many arguments, one night he threw me down on the bed and said, "This time I will fix you so you can't leave me again. No one will ever want you now with two children." We never had a sexual relationship like normal married couples. He forced sex on me again, and instead of using protection, he impregnated me. I was raped by this man again; this man who I thought cared for me hurt me once again. He just wanted me under his thumb, so he could dominate me and my fertile self became pregnant again.

If only I had listened to Mom and Dad, none of these awful things —all the mental abuse and frequent beatings—would have ever happened to me. All alone and bewildered I put up with the awful punishments that he would pound on my body. All I had to do was say something the wrong way and he would start beating me again and again. We hardly had any food. He never gave me any spending money. All Mike had was control over me. All I had was little Anna Maria, and the two of us became very close.

The Comfort of Mom and Dad

Anna and I would take walks together, that is all we could do. Once, I took her and we walked over to the bus stop. I needed to see my parents. I needed their love and comfort. I missed them tremendously. They were surprised to see us. I always tried to hide everything from them, because I did not want to hurt them any more than I already had. When they found out I had taken the bus to see them, they were so happy.

After arriving at their home, they asked me if I was hungry, in the true Italian way. I said I was not hungry, but that I was craving some crabs. Dad, who was the most superstitious person I knew, went right out to Bud's, which was a crab house and restaurant on Lombard Street, not far from their house. Dad had to get some crabs for me because he told me if I did not eat what I wanted while I was pregnant, the baby might be born with a birthmark. He believed in this very strongly, and this was the way he was all of his life.

Mr. Bud's restaurant was near Uncle Mimi's house and the two men were best friends. Dad knew he could get good crabs at Mr. Bud's. When Dad brought the crabs' home, we had a great feast. I stayed with them until evening. When I was with my parents it made me feel content. I had solace when I was with them. After the wonderful day I spent with my parents, Dad drove me back home to that awful place, where I had all those horrible things happen to me.

All I got after this was more and more abuse. One time Mike pushed me down the steps in front of our house where everyone could see him hit me. He screamed and yelled at me to leave him alone because I asked to go out with him. "You can't come with me," he said, and he left me lying there on the ground to pick myself up and go back into the apartment with Anna.

I had no idea what he was doing. I did not know he was going out to buy drugs and when he was in desperate need of them, he was like a maniac. I was tired of being left alone all the time. I just wanted to be treated like a person, not like a child who was being punished for something I had done wrong. I just did not know what I had done to anger him.

He would say, "You can't go where I am going."

Little did I know he was going out to buy heroin. He told me he was going out to sell watches. He said he liked selling watches and that was how he made his money, which I could not understand why he would do this when he was an excellent barber. He said that he hated being a barber. He told me selling watches was so much better, and he could make more money. Of course, I never saw any of it. He would buy food for us, but I could not interfere with anything he was doing, or he would beat me. He never wanted to have anything to do with me. He kept treating me as if I was a child. If I interfered, I would be punished.

One time when we were arguing, I confronted him about staying out all night. He threw me up against the refrigerator door, which was open, and bashed my head into the eggs. They went all over me and the kitchen. Everything got broken, and he ran out of the apartment and left me alone, again with my self-esteem destroyed and Anna who had no idea what was happening. He left me again to clean up all of the mess. He wanted to go out and get his narcotics and be with his friends.

After this incident, I tried to stay out of his way, because I was far into my pregnancy now. I did not want to do anything to hurt the baby that I was carrying. As it turned out, a neighbor who lived upstairs from me was also being beaten by her husband. We became friends. She would watch out for me and I would watch out for her.

Left: Best Man Johnny DiPietro and Vincent DiPietro at Vince's wedding in Brooklyn, Maryland, October 20, 1962. Below: Mike and Peachy in Atlantic City, July 1963.

Fifteen: The Unseen Future

My due date was drawing near for the birth of my second child. It was a cold winter day in February. It had snowed, our furnace had broken, and there was no heat in the apartment. Anna and I walked around all day with our coats on. To make things worse, every time the people in the apartment upstairs flushed their toilet, it would erupt into our toilet and spilled all over the bathroom floor. I was unable to call someone to come and help me because I had no phone. I spent the entire day cleaning the mess in the bathroom. Mike went out leaving me to clean up everything alone again. Before he left, I said to him, "Mike, I don't feel well today; please don't stay out all night because I might have to go to the hospital to have the baby." He went anyway. Later that evening the pains started to come and lasted all through the night.

Suddenly, there came a knock on the door. It was the city workers; they came to fix the toilet and the furnace. I thought, "Oh my God, he really does care about me. He called all of these people to come and fix all the things that were wrong." After they fixed the furnace and the sewage they left, and then the pains came on stronger and stronger. I kept thinking Mike would be home soon because he usually came home at daybreak.

The girl upstairs heard me moaning and came down to help me. She said, "You have got to go to the hospital or you might have the baby right here." She went next door, called my sister-in-law, and asked her to come and take me to the hospital. Once again, I was trying to hide the abuse from my parents. By the time my sister-in-law came to the apartment, I could feel the baby's head wanting to come out. "Hurry up," I said, "I can feel the head coming." I put my hand down there to try to hold the baby from getting hurt. On the ride to the hospital, I felt every bump that my sister-in-law hit. By the time we got to the hospital, I could not even walk. My sister-in-law jumped out of the car and ran to get help.

The nurses came with a wheelchair and swept me into the hospital. In the elevator to the delivery room I started to cry. I had left Anna with my sister-in-law behind the closed elevator door without kissing her goodbye. I was so upset that all I wanted was to hold her in my arms and have Mom's arms around me.

The Unseen Future

And now I was about to bring another child into this world not knowing how I was going to take care of her. Little Michelle was born at Mercy Hospital at 10:30 A.M. on Monday, February 1, 1965. The day before Michelle was born, we had the most terrific snow storm ever. Her little life began in such turmoil that I had no name picked out for her. After all the incidents that had been going on in my life, how could I have done all of the normal things a person does when they are expecting a child? I named her Michelle after her father, and Ann after my grandmother, because she needed someone good in her life.

My parents came up to visit me and they asked me the whereabouts of Mike. They were upset, for they knew that I was in a lot of trouble now, and Mike was not there to help me. The next day, my sister-in-law came to see me at the hospital and told me the dreaded truth that Mike had been locked up again.

I found out Mike had been picked up by the police for selling drugs. After his arrest, he tried to pretend that he was a concerned parent. He told the police all the things that were wrong at the apartment, thinking the police would let him out of jail, but they kept him. They must have believed part of his story though, because they did send all of the city workers over to the apartment to fix everything that was wrong. The police did not fall for his sob story because he was such an exaggerator. He did not fool the police, though, and they kept him locked up.

Mike had such a bad habit that by the time little Michelle was born he was out of control. He could not go for more than three hours before he had to have another fix. When I was released from the hospital, I went to my parents' home because I needed their help with the new baby and Anna. I stayed there for several days in the comfort of my parents and they just loved having me and the children there, as I loved being with them.

Mike got out of jail quickly. I did not understand how he was able to make bail because I surely did not have any money. Later I found out that he turned informant. In other words, he bargained with the police to save himself. He could beat up on me, but he could not face the consequences of being in jail and having to pay for his bad actions. He did not want to be detained in jail because he would not be able to get his drugs. Mike's life was really in danger because he told the cops where some of his suppliers were located. I did not understand what he did, but I soon found out he had put all of us in danger, just to save himself. We were very fortunate that no one found out what he had done, because if they knew what he did, they definitely would have hurt him, and possibly me and the children.

Discovering the Gruesome Truth

When Mike brought me back to the apartment, he finally told me the horrible truth that he had an extremely bad habit. He told me that he had been using heroin all along. I was astonished; I could not believe that he would do this. He told me he would never put a needle in his arm, but his friends showed him how easy it was and then he started to administer the drug to himself. What a gruesome discovery. The only thing I knew about heroin was that it was an addicting drug. I did not know all the side effects that heroin could have on one's body, but I soon found out. I tried to help him kick the habit, not knowing what was in store. It was unbearable, because Mike was in excruciating pain. I would rub his bones with alcohol to try to take some of the pain away and gave him aspirin to help ease his pain, but nothing seemed to help him.

Finally, after several days of trying to help him with his suffering, he started to feel a little better. But, in true addict form, he went right out again to go and buy some more narcotics. After all that I did for days to relieve him of his pain and misery, all he needed was more heroin. He said he was going out to sell watches, so he could make money for me and the children.

Later, I found out that in reality he just wanted to bring his habit down to where he could afford it so he would be able to pay for his narcotics without having to steal money and risk getting arrested again. I could not believe he went back to his same routine. I started to realize that he was so addicted that he did not care about anything but his drugs.

The Spoiled Baptism

I tried to have a little ceremony for Michelle's baptism. It had not even been a month, but Mike was arrested once again. The Saturday night before the baptism, Mike's sister came over to the apartment and told me he was in jail. He did not care about the children, and he certainly did not care about me. He only cared about getting his fix. He could not even be there for his daughter's baptism. The drugs had such a hold on his body that he could not stop himself; they controlled his whole life. What was I going to do? Everything was set up for the baptism. How was I going to face my parents again without upsetting them further? I was so bewildered and too young to realize what to do.

In the morning, my sister came over to the apartment because she was the one I had asked to stand for Michelle. We went to church for the baptism, the priest was very vindictive towards me because my husband was not with me. I practically had to beg him to baptize Michelle. Without any money I could not have any kind of a party afterward. I just took my two little children and went home alone again. I was always trying to cover for Mike. I could have been in the safety of my parents home. When was I going to wake up?

While Michelle was still a baby she became very ill, she threw up and had diarrhea at the same time. I did not want to burden my parents, so I called the only person that I could trust to help my child— old, friendly Dr. Constantini. I explained that I had no money, but asked if he could please help me get my child well. Dr. Constantini told me to buy barley, boil it, and take the broth from the barley and give it to Michelle. He said it would put a lining on her stomach, and she would stop throwing up and it would also stop her diarrhea. It did exactly what the doctor told me it would do.

All I could think of was that I had to get a job so that I could take care of my children. I could not count on Mike for help with anything. I had to take control of the money situation myself. He was never home. I found a job at The Big Boy's restaurant that was all the way on Loch Raven Boulevard, far from where we lived. It was the first restaurant job I had, and I liked it, because it gave me a chance to see the outside world. I had to beg and borrow just to get a ride to work, and then I had to leave my children with people I really did not know and could not trust. When I came home, they were both hungry and needed to be fed and Michelle needed to have her diaper changed.

Finally, my parents stepped in and took me and the children in with them. They had seen enough and wanted to put a stop to the abuse.

When I moved back with my parents, my nerves were getting the best of me, and I thought I was pregnant again. I was very upset. The only person who I could confide in was my cousin Mary Rose. I had to tell someone, and she was the only person who had a situation similar to mine. Her first husband mistreated her terribly. I finally found out that I was not pregnant and that it really was my nerves that made me miss my period. I had enough to do to take care of two children. I did not know what I would have done if I had another child. My cousin helped me through this difficult time. She gave me the confidence that I needed to survive on my own. She had made it, and she had four children. This was a sufficient amount of encouragement to make me go on with my life.

More Abuse

But still, after I was living the safe life with my parents, I went back to Mike. I did not know why I believed his lies, but I did. He would cry and beg me to take him back. "Please, please Leonora," he would say. "Please take me back, I promise I will be different." He told me he loved me, and if I went back with him, he would never hurt me again. He told me he was clean and he had gone back to cutting hair. So again, I believed him and his lies.

He rented a nice apartment with pretty furniture. It was in an apartment development full of young couples our age. We actually almost started to have a social life, making friends with the neighbors. It was really nice for a while. The apartment complex had a swimming pool and the neighbors would have parties there on the weekends. I could take the children wading in the children's pool. Things were going along just fine, and it seemed as if we were having a normal family life.

Then, as before, Mike repeated his old pattern all over again. He just could not stop taking heroin. I finally resigned to the reality that he would never stop taking narcotics. I would just stay with him because I thought I was doing the right thing for the children. I was under the impression that the children needed a father. But when he was in need of his fix he wanted every bit of money that I made each week, and when I would not give it to him, he would start to beat me again.

I could not give the money to him because I needed the money to take care of the children. Once he knocked me on the floor and he was banging my head right near one of the children's toys. He banged my head so hard on the floor that it hit one of the toys, and blood splashed everywhere. This must have scared him because he got off of me and ran out of the apartment and left me alone again, with my bleeding injuries and my children crying hysterically.

Starting to Open My Eyes

It was around this time in the mid-'60s that things in the world were starting to change. The women's movement was gaining steam and women were starting to take a stand for themselves. I started to listen to some of the women at work, and they would tell me I was foolish for putting up with Mike's abuse. Everyone kept asking me, "Why do you stay with Mike, what does he do for you?" They were right. He was worthless. Finally, my eyes were starting to open, and I was learning that women could make it on their own. I could finally leave this horrible man and the miserable life I was leading.

After I left Mike, I had a hard time establishing a life for myself. I tried to buy a car so I could get around town to go to work and take the children out. When I went to the finance company to ask for a loan, they told me that I needed a man's signature on the loan. They said that I had just recently been divorced, and they wanted to see how my payments were going to be made on my bills before they could give me a loan. They told me that I had to prove myself as a reliable person. They wanted to see if I could face my obligations, when all along I was the one who was scraping to pay the bills when I was with Mike. They didn't believe in the strength of a woman.

Peachy's daughters, Michelle Ann and Anna Maria, 1965.

Sixteen: The Turning Point

The turning point in my life came when Mike left the children in the car by themselves while he went to get his fix.

He would take me to work in the morning, and then he was supposed to take the children to Mom's, but on this one morning, he did not. He went to buy heroin with the children still in the car. Not only did he expose the children to this dangerous neighborhood, he left them in the car by themselves for a long time. He went into a house to get his fix, but rather than leaving right away, he took the heroin while in the house.

This was quite a long time to leave the children alone. The car was not in the greatest condition, and Michelle, who was only eight months old, got out of the car seat and started to fool around with the gear shift. She knocked it out of park, and the car started to drift down the hill. A strange man came to their rescue, stopping the car, and saving their lives. I do not even know who this person was so I could thank him for saving my children, but I thank God that he was there to save them.

By the time they got to Mom's, Anna, who was only two then, was extremely upset. When Mom finally got the story out of Anna about what had happened, she called me at work to tell me the ordeal that the children had been through. That was it. I had my epiphany.

The Revelation

How could Mike do this to the children? They were young and unable to help themselves. I had put up with him beating on me and abusing me for years, but this one thing was the revelation that I needed. I should have known better. He did not respect himself and he did not respect me, so how could I ever think he would respect the children? He was so strung out that he did not care about anything or anyone except getting his fix. All along, I kept telling myself that the children needed a father. Yes, they did, but not a father who was a drug addict. I had taken enough grief from him. I knew it was time to leave him for good now. I started planning my move, but I did not have to plan too much, because he was arrested for stealing money to support his habit again that very next weekend. Behind bars, Mike was unable to stop me.

I also made the decision that I was not going to help him get out of jail like I had done in the past. I went to Dad and asked him to lend me money so I would be able to leave Mike. Mom helped me to persuade him, and soon Dad lent me the $500 I needed to move into my own apartment. It was right down the street from my parents. At last, I had somewhere to go where I could do what I wanted, when I wanted, and where I could have the children all to myself. I had peace of mind and I was close to Mom and Dad again. I loved it and so did the children.

I thought that I really needed a change, so off to the nearest drug store I went. I bought a bottle of hair dye, and just like that, I became a redhead. I needed a fresh start, and when I changed my hair color, it made me feel good about myself, something that I had not felt for a very long time. I felt terrific, because I knew right then and there I was going to survive. This was the big turning point in my life.

Divorce Final, Seed Planted

Mom went with me to court to get my divorce. She stood by me through everything, as did the whole family. Uncle Mimi found a lawyer for me and he told him not to charge me a lot. But because I got a cheaper rate, the lawyer felt in his rights to make advances towards me. He told me I had to come to the office late in the evening after everyone had gone home so that he would not have to pay his employees extra. After a few evenings of being chased all around the office by the lawyer, I started taking Mom to the lawyer's office with me. When it was time for the divorce, the lawyer took Mom and me to the judge's chambers, and just like that, the divorce procedures were over in no time at all. All the tragedy that the children and I and my family went through was over in just a few minutes.

Mike did not show up for the proceedings and he never even contested the divorce. I felt I had wasted seven years of my life, and was unable to have someone love me for who I was. Even though I was a strong person, Mike robbed me of my self-confidence. He made me feel that I was incapable of ever having a lasting relationship and I have never found anyone to love me the way Dad loved Mom. I've finally realized the reason Mike treated me so badly was because he simply did not love me.

After the divorce, I hardly heard from Mike. He basically left me alone. Although, every three years, he seemed to remember he had children, and he would call me. He wanted to come around and see us, but I'd had enough of his unpleasantness. I did not believe his lies anymore. I finally woke up to the reality that he would never change because of his horrible addiction to heroin. I had moved on with my life, and I was not about to go back to that awful situation.

I had a job that I loved. I worked in the showroom of Anderson Oldsmobile as secretary to the president, the sales manager, and thirteen salesmen. I also worked the switchboard, and I ordered the cars from the factory. It was great. The only problem was my salary. I only made $55 a week. Even though it was 1965, for all the different jobs that I did at work, I thought I should have been making more money. There was no money left over for anything. I only had enough to pay bills.

There was a restaurant across the street from the car dealership where everyone would go for lunch. I confided in a waitress named Flo (and, yes, she was just like the character from the '70s sitcom) and told her my dilemma. I said to her, "I need money to take care of the children."

She said to me, "Why don't you become a waitress?"

"I don't know the first thing about being a waitress," I said.

She would say, "You can do it; it's easy."

She encouraged me and said, "You are young and pretty and you will do great." Then she said, "After you become a waitress, you will have money in your pocket every day to buy milk, food, and medicine for your children." She was my inspiration and I decided to give waitressing a try.

Mike Visiting the Children

Because Michelle did not look like Anna, and looked more like me, Mike claimed Michelle was not his. This is how his small mind worked. How could he think this of me? I was so afraid of him, I could not get away from the hold he had on me. I would not even think of doing anything with another person. All the things that he did to me, another relationship with someone else was the farthest thing from my mind. He slighted her and I am sure Michelle could feel his belittling attitude.

As the children got older and did not need as much attention, Mike wanted to come to visit them more often. He would take them out, and when he did, he would buy numerous things for Anna and hardly anything for Michelle. One time when he brought them back home, Michelle was in tears because he would not buy her a doll like he bought Anna. I did not want to put her through this ordeal again. After this, I told him he could not take the children out anymore. It was too painful for Michelle, and if he could not treat them equally, he was not going to be able to take the children out at all.

The Demise of Mike

Many years had passed since I left Mike. I made a comfortable life for the children by myself. Suddenly out of nowhere, Mike's brother called me and told me Mike was not going to live much longer. I went to the hospital to visit him, but by the time I arrived, he was comatose. He had abused drugs for such a long time that they had finally taken a toll on his life. He even lost sight in one of his eyes. Within days of visiting him, he passed away. His brother Patrick and sister Juanita asked me to attend his funeral. I brought my daughter Anna, but Michelle was still so upset over the way he treated her that she did not want to attend the funeral. She told me that I had been both mother and father to her and she did not want to see him.

This was one of the worst funerals I have ever attended. The deceased is usually ushered out of the funeral home by pallbearers carrying the casket. Mike, however, was taken out the back door by funeral home employees. After all the times he ran out to be with his friends, not one of them came to his funeral. Even his two brothers, Patrick and Pouche, refused to carry his casket. Mike had done so many bad things to them through the years that they did not want to carry him to his last resting place. When we arrived at the cemetery the gravediggers carried him from the hearse to the gravesite. It was the most depressing funeral I have ever attended. After all of the physical and mental abuse Mike had put me through, this is how his life ended.

Becoming a Waitress

There was an ad in the paper for a waitress at a fancy restaurant downtown, so I went to apply for the job. It was the revolving roof-top restaurant above the Holiday Inn, which overlooked the whole city. Guests at The Circle One restaurant could have a splendid dining experience whiletaking in a beautiful view of the city. To my surprise, I got the job without knowing a thing about being a waitress.

My first day at work, I had to follow someone around so I could learn where everything was. The waitresses taught me about all the different places to go to order the food and drinks. They introduced me to a dup pad, which is a duplicate system that created three copies of a written-up order with one slip going to the kitchen, one to the bartender, and one to the customer. This seemed easy enough to me. On the menu there were special five-course dinners, which included appetizer, soup, salad, main course, dessert, and coffee, all for one reasonable price. Naturally, most of the people who came to the restaurant ordered the five-course dinner.

The first day that I was allowed to work on my own was a Thursday, and everyone I waited on ordered French onion soup. We put croutons and cheese on top of the soup. It looked fabulous. I thought, "Oh, wait until I tell Dad. He will love this because they not only put cheese on their soup, but they also put croutons on their soup." The only soup Mom made was chicken noodle soup, and we always put grated cheese on top of it. Mom's homemade chicken noodle soup was the best.

Mom's Chicken Noodle Soup:

*3 chicken thighs
(deboned and skinless - they have the sweetest   meat)
12 qt. pot of water
1 lge. onion cut in half and then into smaller pieces
8 stalks of celery cut in half, then cut in thirds
preferably with the leaves on – they have more flavor
30 baby carrots peeled – then cut in half
1/3 tsp of pepper
4 tbsp. parsley
1 8 oz. can of tomato puree
1 lb. bag of egg noodles
2 cans chicken broth
Cook the chicken in the water; and pepper and chicken broth,
and cook for one hour on a low flame. Add the vegetables, and
cook for another hour. Add the tomato puree, and cook for another hour. In a pot of boiling water, cook the egg noodles until
tender. Strain the noodles. Remove the chicken and shred it. Put
the chicken back into the soup and add the noodles. Add grated
parmesan cheese to your taste. Serves 6.*

The First Big Mistake

The next day was Friday, and everyone I waited on ordered clam
chowder. All of my customers got croutons and cheese on top of
their clam chowder.

At the end of the evening, one of the customers said to his wife,
"Honey, I thought we ordered clam chowder."

I replied, "Oh, you did sir. We put croutons and cheese on it here."

Just then another waitress walked by and said, "Leonora, you
don't put croutons and cheese on clam chowder." All night long, the
other waitresses laughed at me. I felt so foolish. I thought I would
never learn how to be a waitress...you have to remember too much!

The Excitement of Being a Waitress

We also had a bartender who was extremely nasty to me. Instead
of helping me to get the customers waited on more efficiently, he

made a complete fool out of me. What did I know about drinks? Nothing. All Dad ever drank was beer and some wine or anisette on special occasions. I did not know anything about martinis or Manhattans, which I found out later everyone would order before dinner. I did not know what went in them, or what "rocks," "straight up," or "neat" meant.

I went to the bar to order my drinks, and the bartender said, "Do they want it up or on the rocks?"

I said, "I don't know."

He then said to me, "Go back and ask the customer!"

As I went back to find out how the customers wanted their drinks, I forgot that the restaurant was revolving so it took me a while to find the customer. When I got back to the bartender, I had to wait my turn in line again.

When my turn finally came to deal with the bartender, he said, "Do they want an olive, onions, or a twist?"

I said, "I don't know."

And back I went to ask the customer. By now, the restaurant was all the way around to the other side, and I was running to find the customers. When I finally caught up to them, they must have thought that I was really a bad waitress. Needless to say, everything went downhill from there.

My first Saturday night at Circle One was a disaster. I lost the dup pad for my orders and I did not know what to do. I was so upset that I went and hid in the linen closet and cried my eyes out. Whatever made me think I could be a waitress? All I wanted to do was run out of the restaurant, but before I could escape the manager found me.

He was such a nice German man, and he went to every one of my tables and said to the customers, "Please bear with us for a little while. The waitress is new, but if you will be a little patient, I will make sure that you get your dinner, okay?" He stayed with me throughout the entire evening. He showed me the proper way to serve the customers and he showed me how to crumb the table, something else that I did not know about. He said to me, "Always flatter the women, because if you try to flatter the men, the wives will get jealous. You are young and pretty, and the men will like you anyway, but if you get the women on your side, then you will have the whole table in sync with you." I made it through the evening, plus I made some money, and I was loving life.

There was a little man who worked in the kitchen who seemed to wash the kitchen floor every few minutes. The uniforms that we wore were sparkling white. I would go into the kitchen running because I was always in a hurry while serving the customers. And often I would slip on the wet floor and fall on my rear end, sliding all the way over to the ice-cream box that was on the other side of the room. By the end of the evening, my white uniform was usually black. Everything I had served was all over me. I was trying to be more efficient, but it was very difficult because I still was unclear about what I was doing.

My shy Mom did not like to go to restaurants because she did not want people to watch her eat. I never understood what she meant until I became a waitress. When you are a waitress, you have to watch your customers to see if they need anything. This is the reason why she did not want to go out to eat. When she worked at John Hopkins serving the nurses, she had to watch their every move to see if they needed anything. I finally understood what Mom meant about having people watch you eat.

As time went by, I became a pretty good waitress and I was making some extra money. I was able to do things for my children and pay my bills, and I was happy. I still did not have a car, but it did not seem to matter because I took cabs everywhere or got rides with people. But many times, I found myself standing on the corner waiting for a bus in all kinds of inclement weather.

I kept my day job at the car dealership for two and a half more years so that I could afford to send my daughters to Catholic school to get a good education. It was expensive, but I knew this was the most important thing that I could do for them. If they did not have a good education, they would not be able to get ahead in life.

At Circle One, there was one waitress who treated me as her equal. Perhaps it was because we had so much in common. She was a single mother who was also struggling to raise two young children on her own. She was a little older and more experienced, but she never laughed at me. She only helped me out whenever I fouled up.

Jean was a tall, gorgeous, elegant blonde. Guys would always notice her. When she walked into a room full of men they would all look her way because she had a terrific figure. In the summer, she took her children on trips in her car and she asked me and my girls to go along. Once, we took all the children to Ocean City for a few days. We did not have much money, but we had lots of fun! As all young people did in the '60s, we spent our days on the beach and our nights on the boardwalk eating frozen custard and fries, laughing, scratching our sunburned skin, and taking the children to the rides on the pier. It was nice to have a rest from work and worry and to see the children having a good time. Providing this time for my little girls made me feel responsible. Of course, sometimes things would not go right, but during the good times, it made me feel happy that I could take care of my children on my own.

Across Lombard Street from the Holiday Inn was a big arena called the Baltimore Civic Center. The NBA Bullets played basketball there, the Baltimore Clippers played hockey there, the circus took place there, and big stars performed concerts there. One night in 1965, Frank Sinatra came to the arena to perform. We were extremely busy at the restaurant. Most of the people came in the restaurant for dinner and then went across the street to see the show. I never saw Frank myself, but I saw his limousine pull out of the arena. The celebrity entrance and exit was on the side facing the Holiday Inn. Everyone was at the window watching him pull away. We were ten stories up, and he was down below in his limousine driving off to the airport. It wasn't as though he really could see us or we could really see him, but for us it was big excitement.

A few weeks later, on a Sunday afternoon, I arrived at work to find several police cars out in front of the hotel. The staff had to go in the back entrance. When we got inside, we learned that a woman had jumped to her death from the restaurant's roof. She had gone onto the balcony of the restaurant and had hidden until the restaurant closed. Then she jumped, landing on the awning below. After this horrible event, the balcony was kept locked. Visitors could no longer enjoy the beautiful view from the rooftop garden.

After working at the Holiday Inn for a couple of years, I wanted to get a car. I really could not take my children to places alone. I always had to depend on someone else taking us. I had deprived my children of a normal childhood because I had to work so much, and I wanted to be able to do something special for them. I was trying to be an independent person and I felt I needed a car to be able to really be independent.

The Driver's License

Dad would not teach me how to drive. He was afraid if I had a car, I would have an accident and hurt myself. I went through nine learner's permits because no one would teach me how to drive. Finally, I decided to hire a driving instructor to teach me. The instructor was a nice, middle-aged man. There was only one drawback; no one would watch the children for me while I took the driving lessons.

My parents were so against my driving that for the first time in my life they refused to do something for me and watch the kids. I told the instructor the only way I could take the lessons was if I could bring my children with me.

He said, "This is not allowed, young lady."

I said, "Oh, well, I just won't be able to take the lessons." I begged and begged until finally he changed his mind, and he told me I could bring them if they behaved. So I told Anna and Michelle that if they wanted me to take them places, they would have to be quiet while I learned how to drive. The girls sat in the back seat as quiet as mice.

After nine learner's permits, I finally passed the test with flying colors and got my driver's license. Now all I needed to do was buy a car. Easier said than done!

Seventeen: The Golden Arm

The girls I worked with at Circle One started talking about a new restaurant that would be opening up just a few blocks north of the city line. It would be owned by the one-and-only Johnny Unitas, Hall of Fame quarterback for the Baltimore Colts, and his partner, Bobby Boyd, who was one of the strongest defensive players on the team. One day while I was working at the car dealership, a huge sign on the back of a truck suddenly rode down the street. It was Johnny U's arm, famously cocked to release a long bomb pass, on its way to be installed on the front of his new restaurant. I was superstitious enough to see the sign as an omen for me to go there and apply for a job. So off I went on my lunch break to Johnny U's restaurant. People were still working on the restaurant when I went inside. As I passed one of the construction workers, I overheard him say "She's pretty, I would hire her." To my surprise, I was hired.

Johnny and Bobby's restaurant had a rough opening with many kinks and glitches. During the first weekend the toilet in the ladies room was all blocked up, and in walked Johnny U with a plunger to fix the problem. The women were flabbergasted. They did not know what to do except to laugh. Where else could you go and have the famous Johnny Unitas fix your toilet?

Johnny had piercing eyes that could look right through you, and he could find your inner feelings and, oh, when he flashed his smile, it would light up the whole room. With such a charismatic personality, he had you in the palms of his hands.

Once the kinks were ironed out, everything started to run smoothly at the restaurant. In the lobby was a brick floor and a coat-check room, with the hostess desk up front. The front room was a long aisle with tables and booths. At the end of the aisle hung a huge picture of #19 with his bow legs (just like my father's!) walking off the field. The bar was over to the left, with bar stools and tables. It had two of the most humorous bartenders, Rocky and Jimmy, who told jokes and had the customers laughing all the time. The next room had a piano bar with stools around the piano, large booths, and four tables. On the weekend, a handsome young man played requests on the piano. I would ask him to sing my favorite song—"I'm Looking for an Angel," which I have been all of my life.

The main dining room had huge plaques of all the players' helmets with their numbers on them. The coffee station, bathrooms, and kitchen were in the rear of the restaurant.

They served steaks and prime rib that were so tender you could cut them with a fork. They also had lobster and surf-and-turf, crab cakes, soups and salads, and the most wonderful thing that I was introduced to—Jack Tar potatoes. This delight was a baked potato split open with the inside dug out, mashed with butter, and mixed with grated cheese, parsley, bacon bits, and sour cream before being scooped back into the skins and re-baked. They were simply marvelous. It is one of the most delicious things I have ever eaten.

The Tragedy

During the football season we were always busy, but during summer time business slowed down. People went on vacation and famous football players were the farthest thing from their minds. One slow summer Sunday evening, young thugs came in the restaurant to rob it, but after they looked around and saw all the people that were in the restaurant, they left quickly. When they left Johnny's they headed to the nearby sub shop on the strip mall. There, in the course of a robbery, they shot one of the teenage employees in the head and then fled. The other kids came running to our restaurant for help. We brought linens to wrap the poor boy's bleeding head. We tried to keep him comfortable until help arrived, but it was no use and the young boy died from his wound.

After this incident, the slack summer business dwindled to almost nothing. It was a good thing I kept my day job at the car dealiership. Even though it did not pay a lot, it was something to help me with the bills.

Working two jobs took me away from the children for long periods of time. I felt so guilty for leaving them while I was working those long hours. So when I was off, I spent all of my spare time with them.

Eventually my friend Jean from Circle One came to work at Johnny U's. We spent the summer taking our children to Ocean City and nearby beaches and on picnics. We would pack a lunch and go on day trips with the children, spending the whole day with them watching them have fun.

Bobby's Theory

To help improve business, Bobby Boyd told us to charge the Colts players half price for their dinners. When people found out all the Colts players were coming to the restaurant on a regular basis, crowds returned. We were always busy after this. After home games all of the Colts went to Johnny U's for dinner and brought their wives. Tom Matte, Bill Curry, Mike Curtis, Jimmy Orr, and Alex Hawkins came often to eat. I would have to hide from Alex Hawkins when he came into the restaurant. He was always asking me to go out. I would be at the bar getting drinks for the customers and when he saw me he would say, "Hey, big reds, when are you going to give me a break?" When he said this, I would go and hide in the kitchen. Bobby's wife would also come in after the games to be with him, and Johnny's wife would be there also as did most of the other Colts players and their wives. Eventually, all the guys would wind up sitting around one table and talking about the game, laughing, and telling jokes. So you see, eventually Bobby's theory did work. Sometimes, the older Colts players would come in the restaurant, like Alan Ameche, Gino Marchetti, and Lenny Moore. Mr. Rosenbloom, the owner of the Colts, would also be there.

My Sister's Wedding

In 1969, Rosie met a guy named Bernie. Bernie was short, thin, and kind of cute with bushy hair and glasses.

I said, "Rosie, there is no meat on his body; you will have to bring him over to the house so Mom can give him some of her home cooking. That should fatten him up real good."

After having dinner at Mom and Dad's one night, Bernie said to Rosie, "Does your family always fight like that?"

Rosie said, "They weren't fighting, they were only expressing themselves." Our Italian family was always very excitable, and when we expressed our emotions it seemed to other people that we would be fighting. All along we were not, we were all a very loving family.

Rosie started to plan her wedding. Dad told me to ask off from work early to make sure that I would be able to attend the wedding. He did not want anything to go wrong because Rosie was his baby girl. Dad and Mom were very excited. Mom wanted everything to be perfect for Rosie because they were always extremely close. Mom wanted to do for Rosie what she could not do for me. Rosie had lots of bridesmaids, and Bernie had a lot of brothers, everything turned out just perfect, and all of the bridesmaids wore yellow. Rosie had become a fantastic beautician; she would always work on Mom's and my hair and fix our hair in exotic styles. On her wedding day, Rosie fixed everyone's hair; she wanted all of us to look beautiful.

Rosie was so gorgeous on her wedding day, and she and Bernie had a lovely church ceremony, followed by a reception at a huge hall in Overlea. It was such a perfect church wedding, with flowers, a band, a huge cake, and the whole family together once again. Everyone danced until late in the evening. Mom later told Rosie this was one of the happiest times of her life, because it was the last time the whole family was all together. After this, the older generation began dying off.

Dad was so proud of how the wedding reception turned out, that he went around to all of the tables which were full of all our relatives, and told them to make sure that they ate plenty of food and to drink up because he had paid for everything, and he wanted to make sure that he got his money's worth.

Going Back To Work

After summer was over and football season began, Sundays at Johnny U's were crazy! There would be specials running every Sunday, and we had buses taking people to the stadium, which would bring the people back to Unitas' after the game. So, the restaurant would be busy before and after the game.

Now that the Colts players and their wives and friends would come into the restaurant after the game, it would be so crowded that it was hard to maneuver around all the tables. The bar and the dining rooms were packed. Bobby Boyd treated his fellow players great when they came into the restaurant. When the Colts won, it would be busy until two o'clock in the morning.

Walking on the Moon

I worked at Johnny U's when this historical event happened. Everyone was there in front of the large TV that the restaurant had in the bar room on July 20, 1969, when the Americans walked on the moon. We couldn't believe this amazing part of history was unfolding right before our eyes. Everybody was glued to the TV. No one ever thought this could happen during our lifetime. Vince, who was working at Goddard Space Center then, was on cloud nine. He had always told us that one day a man would walk on the moon.

Neil Armstrong, who was the first astronaut to walk on the moon, made this historical statement, "One small step for man, one giant leap for mankind."

Dad—who was glued to the TV, too, at the house—thought it was a miracle. He said to mom, "Phil, the next thing they're going to do is sell bottled water." Little did he know this, too, would come to be true. Dad was mesmerized. Back then, the TV was the link to everything, because it brought all the current events right before your eyes.

The Telethon

Millions of people tuned in to the Jerry Lewis telethon for muscular dystrophy every year. Jerry would have many stars on the show, and they would all donate money to this worthy cause. Thousands of people would call in and donate money for Jerry's Kids. Jerry Lewis raised hundreds of thousands of dollars to find a cure for this horrible disease. He brought everyone's attention to muscular dystrophy. At the end of the show he sang this beautiful song called "You'll

Never Walk Alone." Jerry Lewis and everyone watching in the audience and on TV were crying.

On one of Jerry's shows, Frank Sinatra made an appearance to raise money for Jerry's Kids. Frank got Dean Martin to come on the show at the same time. Frank was the only person who brought Jerry Lewis and Dean Martin together, face to face, to talk to each other again, after all the years that they had been apart. Frank got Dean and Jerry to make up right on national television in front of millions of people.

My two bosses, Johnny and Bobby, also contributed large sums of money to the cause, but since they both were private men, they requested that all of their contributions be anonymous.

The Super Bowl

While I worked at Johnny U's, the Colts made it all the way to the Super Bowl. During the 1968 season, Johnny was playing pick-up football with some of his friends, including Rocky Thorton, the bartender. While playing, Johnny fell into a hole in the ground and damaged his Achilles tendon. He could not play for the rest of the season, so backup quarterback Earl Morrall took over for him. He led the Colts all the way to the Super Bowl against the New York Jets with Joe Namath at quarterback. Broadway Joe went on national television the night before the game and boasted how he was going to win the Super Bowl. Baltimore fans were upset because they thought the Colts were the better team. The Baltimore Colts were our home team and everyone loved them. The Jets were a young team, and no one thought they would win.

On the day of the Super Bowl, the restaurant was full of arrogant people from New York. They sat at the bar all day long and antagonized us. They kept saying the Jets were going to win the Super Bowl, and they cheered for the Jets throughout the whole game, just to aggravate the Baltimore fans and employees at the restaurant. The Colts had a chance to come back and win when they put Johnny U in towards the end of the game. If only they had put Johnny U in sooner because he knew how to work the clock. He would throw sideline passes to the receivers, and then they would run out of bounds, and this would stop the clock. The Colts simply ran out of time, the clock ran out and the Jets won the game.

The people from New York were ecstatic. They were screaming and yelling and upsetting everyone more and more.

When I asked them, "Why did you come here, when Baltimore is such a big town, you could have gone anywhere?"

Their reply was this, "We picked Johnny U's on purpose."

When Johnny U came back from the Super Bowl loss to the Jets, I asked him, "Why didn't you go in the game sooner?"

"I didn't want to take the glory away from Earl," he replied.

That is just the way he was, a very humble man. When Johnny got in the game, he tried hard to make the Colts win, but there just was not enough time.

The Friendly Customers

The restaurant had many great customers. It was as if you were going to your second home. You did not even feel like you were going to work, because something new and fun was always happening. Many customers became repeat customers and they became good friends with Johnny U and Bobby. The Federicos, a father and son lawyer team, would come in every day after court. There was another group of men who came in just about every day for lunch to sit at a round table and discuss their business and the problems of the day. They treated all of us waitresses as if we were part of their family. There would also be celebrities coming in the restaurant. Jim Neighbors came in one time and sang to the customers.

There was a special customer who came into Unitas' every night. He sat at the bar drinking Arrow 77 beer along with Johnny, who considered the man his mentor. Johnny's father died very young, so Mr. Foley became Johnny's father figure. Mr. Foley had an outgoing personality and was the perfect balance for Johnny's introverted personality. Mr. Foley gave Johnny comfort around crowds; he was the gatekeeper for the star quarterback. Mr. Foley always had good things to say about people, he would always say, "Hello, lad." He made you feel comfortable and he extended that comfort to Johnny, and Johnny was like a magnet to Mr. Foley.

The Golden Arm was like a neighborhood bar and everyone would come there just to hang out with Johnny. Wherever Johnny was, Mr. Foley was always in the background. He would always give Johnny support because people were always coming up to him telling him what a great quarterback he was. Johnny was bashful and shy, but Mr. Foley would always give him support, and try to get him to overcome his shyness.

My First Car

I met a man who came in the restaurant and he had a friend that had a used car lot. I asked him if his friend had a cheap car I could buy. The car I bought had been owned by an ex-cop who had wired it up so no one could start it but him. I had to get a hot shot to start the car every time. The only good thing about the car was it only cost me $300. I finally found a way to start the car. I would open the hood of the car and have to take off the air filter, and I would have to let little Anna turn the key while I held the choke down. I had to start the car this way all the time, until I finally got enough money to fix it.

Nevertheless, I finally had a car, and it really did not matter what I had to do to get it started. I would not have to take cabs or buses during inclement weather ever, ever again, and I could take the children out. At this time there was a song out by Stevie Wonder called, "You Are the Sunshine of My Life," and when I took the children out I would sing it to them all the time while I driving them around town. I was extremely happy then.

The Accident

After spending another $300 to finally get my car fixed so I would not have to go under the hood every time I had to start the car, I had an accident. One night I was driving all the busboys home. I felt sorry for them because I remembered how awful it was to wait for a bus on the corner. I only had one more busboy to drop off when I turned up this huge street, and I was not paying attention to what I was doing. Instead, I was putting a cigarette out in the ashtray and not watching where I was going. Before I knew it, I had hit a parked car, and while trying to get away from the parked car, I jerked the wheel. The next thing I knew the car flipped over on its side, slid, and hit another parked car, leaving me and the busboy lying there on our sides in the street. Because it made such a horrible sound, the neighbors heard the crash and came running outside to help us. The neighbors told me to turn the car off, because if I let the car run it would catch on fire. The neighbors were so kind that they helped me and the busboy out of the car. If it had not been for them coming to our aid, the car would have caught fire with us in it.

My driving instructor had told me to always stay on the right side of the road so other people could pass, and I listened to his instructions. I was just recalling what he had told me, and this is why I drove so close to the parked car and had the accident. The street was so huge, if I had been in the middle, I would not have hit the parked cars. I do not know what the busboy was thinking because the accident happened on his side. He could have warned me that I was getting close to the parked cars, but he did not say a thing.

The busboy was a nervous wreck, and when he got out of the car, he ran all the way home. He would not even come to the hospital with me to be checked out. He told me he was all right. He acted as if he had done something wrong.

I just needed a few stitches, but I had bruises all over my body. When my parents found out about the accident, they were extremely upset. Dad almost passed out when he saw me, and when he saw the car, he could not believe that I was alive. He did not say anything negative to me about the accident. He cared for me so much, he was just happy that I was alive.

When I woke up the next day, I had two black eyes, stitches on my face, and a big bruise on my forehead. The doctor told me to put an ice pack on my forehead and the bump would go away. Oh, it went away all right. The huge bulge on my forehead went down to my eyes. My eyes turned black and blue and protruded. I looked like a raccoon. I was a mess.

My car was demolished, and so was my only source of pleasure, the ability to take Anna and Michelle out. I was out of work for almost three weeks with no income. In the meantime, my birthday came along, and the girls from work wanted to take me out because they felt sorry for me. I did not want to go, because I had two huge black eyes, but they insisted. Everywhere we went, people would make fun of me. They would say, "Who hit you in the eye?" I just wanted to go home, but the girls insisted we were going to stay out and have some fun. Maybe they had fun, but I just wanted to go home. When I finally got back to work, I had to take buses and cabs again. I hated it. The insurance I had did not cover the repairs on my car, because the car was not worth anything. I never received any money for the demolished car.

What another mess I got myself into.

Peachy, Johnny Unitas, and the waitresses at The
Golden Arm on May 7, Johnny's birthday (c. 1970).

Top: Rosie and Bernie Jubb in front of 3510 Claremont Street, May 1970. Above: Peachy, Mr. Foley, and unknown friend at The Golden Arm. Right: Michelle and Anna dressed for school, June 1971.

Eighteen: Good Friends

I met three girls while working at Johnny U's in 1969, and we are still friends today. Marge, who was older than I was, had worked in various restaurants throughout Baltimore all of her life to support her five children, and when she came to Johnny U's we became close friends.

My Friend Marge

Marge's oldest son Charles was drafted into the service. Charles was a tall and handsome young man. There was a war going on in Vietnam, and thousands of young men were being killed. Charles was the only one of Marge's children who could have helped her with some of her expenses, but instead he was sent over to Vietnam to fight in one of the worst wars in history. Charles was made a sergeant because he was a natural born leader. While he was leading his platoon, they came upon a land mine. Charles told his men to go back, but when they tried to retreat, the mine exploded. Here was this nineteen-year-old child leading other nineteen-year-old children in this horrible war.

Charles lost both of his legs and his right arm. He was trying to protect his men when this awful thing happened to him. Marge was heartbroken. We did not know what to do to help her or her son. Charles' life was destroyed, and he almost lost his mind after this awful ordeal. Charles ran the streets at night in his wheelchair, and drank himself into oblivion. What could you say, what could you do to help this child? He was extremely distraught and rightly so.

The Vietnam War was unpopular at home, and the Vietnamese people did not want us Americans there either. Young people were staging protests all over America. They were burning their draft cards, and American flags. They were moving to Canada to escape the draft. It was an unsettled time in America.

It took many years for Charles to get his life back together. He was just a child then, but he is a man now, and he has turned his life around. He has made a wonderful life for himself and is now married to a lovely woman. Charles has a car with special devices that enable him to drive it. He has a good job, and he takes excellent care of his mother. He takes care of her finances and has moved her into a subsidized living home. He also takes her shopping and to her many doctor appointments. My friend, Marge, worked all of her life to support her five children alone. Marge does not get enough money from Social Security to live off of today, and her income was never enough for her to save for her old age, which is why she is still working at age 90.

My Friend Rita

My friend Rita was in the same predicament as I was, because she had four boys to support. Although she did get help from her ex-husband, it was still hard raising four boys on her own. Rita and I became good friends. Rita was a beautiful, short redhead with a great figure. Men always wanted to talk to her, because she was a very intelligent person. Rita was the one who could easily strike up a conversation with someone; she was well educated and was very diplomatic about every situation that would arise.

One of the bartenders at Unitas' told us about a club called the Wishing Well, which would be opening soon. He told us that all of the waitresses and bartenders would be going there, because a bartender was going to be one of the owners. Rita told me the club was just down the hill from her house. It was packed every night, and it had a live band every evening. Some of the bands that played there included Al Madman Baitch, Teddy Bell Revue, Tony D. Quintet featuring Louie D., Tommy Vann and the Echo's, Al Rossi, Louie Voir, The High Hopes, and Jimmy Oronson. What a terrific place this was. The Wishing Well had three bars inside and a large dance floor. Rita and I would go there to relax and wind down the evening by re-hashing what happened at Johnny U's that night. After we were there for a while, our friend Jean would come to meet us. I loved to dance, and Rita liked to talk, and eventually our fellow waitresses and bartender friends also joined us there. Two of the bartenders who worked at Johnny U's also worked at the Wishing Well. Rita and I always did a lot of wishing at the well. Rita and I have been friends through many years together, raising our children the best way that we knew how. Through the good times and the bad times, we have remained close.

My Friend Jean

My third friend, Jean, was the hostess with the most fabulous personality. She was short, thin, and blonde. She knew how to talk to people with diplomacy. I was always the bashful one. Jean was also divorced, raising a child alone. But Jean had an ex-husband who helped her with her expenses. Jean always took good care of us, and she made sure the customers took good care of us also. Jean was like our Mother Superior because she would always watch over us. Her mother watched my children sometimes when I didn't have a baby sitter or when my parents were not available. Everyone called her Nana; she was a nice elderly lady. Nana had salt and pepper hair and blue eyes. She fed us and treated the children and me as if we were part of her family.

The four of us have been friends since the '60s. One thing that kept us together through all of these years is that all of our birthdays are in November. Every November we pick a day and go out to celebrate our birthdays at lunch. We call ourselves the "Golden Girls" now. We have also celebrated every Saint Patrick's Day since we worked at Johnny U's. The restaurant always had a huge celebration on March 17 with corned beef and cabbage as a special that was reasonably priced. There would be a line of people waiting in the lobby to get the food at the great price of $3.17. Of course, they also wanted to see Johnny U and Bobby Boyd.

Later on in life, I found out that Saint Patrick's parents were actually Roman, which allowed this Italian Catholic to celebrate along with the Irish. My three girlfriends and I would go to lunch every Saint Patrick's Day to celebrate and reminisce about our days at The Golden Arm.

One time our manager tried to dye our aprons green on Saint Patrick's Day, but he didn't decide to do this until it was almost time for lunch to begin. Can you imagine this, all of our aprons were hanging up over top of pots of boiling water that the manager had tried to dye in the kitchen. All his trouble was in vain, though, because all of our blue aprons never turned green.

Going to the Ocean

During the summer, I usually took the children to the ocean. I love the ocean, it is close to home, and when you are there, it makes you feel so relaxed, probably because the water has a calming effect. It is my favorite place to visit. I worked at restaurants all of my life, and I knew a lot of people who had businesses in Ocean City. I would always find a place to stay that was in my price range, so I could spend more money having fun with the children. Sometimes we would go with my friends and their children, and we would always have a fantastic time. We would even bring food, so we didn't have to eat out all the time and we could afford to take the children on rides on the boardwalk, which they loved.

Acquiring a Loan to Buy a Car

My friend Marge took me to Rose Shanis to get a loan to buy a car. The place would give loans to anybody for a price, but they were especially interested in making loans to women. The interest rate was exorbitant, but I didn't mind. Buying a car was the only thing that mattered to me. Marge took me around to look for a car, and I found a beautiful blue 1958 Chevy Impala with a beautiful white interior. The only thing wrong with the car was that it had lots of miles on it. I did not realize that a car with this many miles on it probably had something wrong with it.

When Dad found out about the car with all those miles that it had on it, he was furious.

He went to the dealership and said to the man, "How could you sell my daughter a car with 150,000 miles on it?"

The manager replied, "It is too late to cancel the deal because the deal has already gone through."

Dad would always say, "Girl, I don't know how you are going to make enough money to pay all of your bills." He would always call me the dollar-down girl. He would say, "Dollar down, dollar when you catch me, this is how you pay people." What Dad didn't realize was that I only had so much money that I had to stretch an extremely long way. This is one thing I have done all of my life. Being a waitress, you can only make so much money. You have good days and bad days, so you can only spread the money as far as it will stretch.

The Blow Out

Before I left for the beach, I checked my car. It was a constant battle to stay ahead of the oil leak that the car had, and I wanted to make sure we could make the trip safely.

Dad said, "You better get the tires checked before you go to the ocean."

I said, "Dad, I don't have enough money to buy tires and take the children to the ocean too. I can only do one or the other."

I chose going on the trip, of course, instead of getting tires. I brought a baby sitter with us so my friend and I could have a little nightlife, also. The baby sitter didn't mind, because I was paying her way to everywhere she went. I had bought a turtle for Anna and Michelle, because they wanted a pet, and naturally, it had to come with us to the ocean. We made it over the Bay Bridge fine, and all of a sudden, one of my tires had a blow- out. The car would not stop. I panicked and stepped on the brake.

When I did this, the car swerved to the right. I know God was with us, because no one was in the other lane, and no one hit our car. Had there been another car in the other lane, we would have surely hit it. There were no seat belts then, and all the windows were open, because the car did not have air conditioning. If we had been hit, we would all have been thrown out of the car and possibly been killed.

I have always carried a statue of the Blessed Mother in the glove box; I always need Her with me (She is still in my glove box today). The statue was with us that day when this accident occurred. Still, my nerves were shot. After the car finally stopped, someone pulled over to help us. I was relieved because I could not move. I was grateful to my rescuers because there was no way I could have gotten behind the wheel after this ordeal. It took over an hour for the people to fix the tire, and that was a miracle in itself. We had to remove all the luggage from the trunk to get to the spare tire. This was another time I should have listened to Dad and didn't. When was I ever going to learn?

In those days, there were no cell phones, so my girlfriend, who was driving separately, didn't know what had happened to me. I had no way of getting in touch with her either. She thought I had changed my mind and was not going to meet her down the ocean. By the time we got there, the day was almost over, but at least we were all safe, and we could spend the rest of our vacation safe and happy together.

While we were at the beach, the children had such a marvelous time because I could be with them the whole time. I worked so much that when we were together we would savor all our time together. Our vacation turned out to be a fantastic one. There was a place on the boardwalk that had a fabulous jukebox. During this period in 1970, two popular top ten songs were out. One was "Young Girl" by Gary Puckett and the Union Gap, and the other was "This Guy's in Love" by Herb Alpert and the Tijuana Brass. Because they would listen to the radio often, Anna and Michelle loved these songs, and I did, too. When we went to the restaurant for lunch, they ran to the jukebox to play the songs over and over again. They could relate to both of these songs because they were going to be young ladies soon themselves.

"Golden Girls" Marge Mason, Rita Scheeler, Peachy Dixon, and Jean Weisner enjoy another lunch together remembering their days at The Golden Arm.

Nineteen: Road to the Super Bowl

*T*he Baltimore Colts were having an exceptional year while I was working at Unitas' in 1971. They were headed to the Super Bowl. A few Sundays before they went to the championship game, legendary Green Bay Packers quarterback Bart Starr came into the restaurant. He sat down at the piano bar and sang "You've Got the Whole World in Your Hands" to Johnny U. Johnny was such a great man; down to earth, humble, and sincere. Everyone loved him, even the players on opposing teams.

My Big Idea

Sidney Omarr wrote the horoscopes for the Baltimore Sun. His predictions were so accurate that I based my day on what he predicted. I wanted to go to the Super Bowl, but I had two children, and very little income. I had an idea though that if I borrowed $1 from everyone I knew, it would be much easier for me to pay them back, but also no one would miss a dollar. Maybe they would miss five, ten, and twenty dollars, but who would miss a dollar at this time? Around this same time, Mr. Omarr wrote the horoscope for me this one day. It read like this, "You are going to make an important decision, and your friends are going to help you out." When I read this, I saw it as a sign that encouraged me to go ahead with my plans to go to the Super Bowl.

I called Clara and said, "Clara that's it, I'm going to do it. We're going to go to the Super Bowl." I started borrowing $1 from everyone I knew: waitresses, bartenders, friends, and relatives. I was able to borrow $1 from one hundred and thirty-eight different people, and only had to pay $6 back. Every time I tried to give the money back, the people would say, "Oh Leonora, you keep the money, we just wanted you to have a good time."

I continued with my plans to go to the Super Bowl. First, I had to find someone to watch the children. I called Vince and told him about my plans. I asked him if he would watch my children, while I went to see the Super Bowl in Florida. Vince agreed to take care of the children. He lived alone, he could use someone to keep him company, and he loved my children so. His wife had left him three years ago, and he was feeling very low since this happened. My wonderful brother loved his wife so and took such good care of her, and after the beautiful wedding that they had, she packed up and left him. We helped each other out through our many different obstacles.

I knew if I told Mom and Dad, they would have all kinds of excuses why I shouldn't go to Florida, although I was only going to be away for two days. They were both conservative, and they would not want me to go because they were always worrying that something was going to happen to me.

Clara worked in a beauty shop, and there was this nice guy named Gene who was a beautician working at the shop. He was hysterically funny. He would always play tricks on the customers, and all the customers loved him. He was our friend. Gene made a huge sign for Clara and me to take to Florida, and it said, "Fly the Friendly Skies of Unitas"; we took this sign on the airplane with us.

Vince and the children took us to the airport to see us off to Florida. After I kissed them all goodbye, Clara, me and one of her friends left for Florida. At the last minute Clara's friend decided she wanted to come with us because her boyfriend had gone down to Florida with his friends. Clara's friend was upset that he had left without her, and she insisted that she had to go and find him. She wanted to be with him.

I had already gotten two tickets for Clara and me from Bobby Boyd. He was one of the strongest defensive players on the team. He had muscles like Popeye, only larger. The tickets that we bought for the Super Bowl only cost $30 a piece then, and the seats were terrific, on the thirty yard line, to be exact. We tried to get an extra ticket for Clara's friend before we left for Florida, but to no avail. We had to sneak her into the room, because when we rented the room it was only supposed to be for two people. One of my customer's brothers was the manager of the hotel in Miami and had gotten the room for us in Florida at a reasonable price. The hotel was right across the street from the ocean, and the rooms were not as expensive as the oceanside hotels were.

One of Clara's friends picked us up from the airport in Miami. The streets of the city were lined with beautiful palm trees. It was the first time I had seen live palm trees. What a gorgeous sight it was. After we checked into the hotel, we rented a car to get around town. When we got back to the hotel, Clara's friend realized that she unconsciously left her purse in the car. By the time we got back to the rental car place, the purse was gone along with all of her money. We told the girl not to worry; we would make sure that she would eat. The hotel was already paid for, we had a car to drive around in, and Clara and I had tickets for the Super Bowl. We really didn't need anything else except a ticket for Clara's friend.

I drove everywhere, because Clara drove at a snail's pace. We also had no clue where we were going, and found everything by accident. I don't know how we managed it, but we got into the parade. The guys put us on a float to wave at the people who had lined the streets to watch the parade. Of course, you have to understand, we were both thinner then. Clara had beautiful blonde hair and I had long red hair. Everywhere we went guys would offer to help us find our way to where we were supposed to go. We traveled all over Florida. We discovered that the bars stayed open until 6 A.M., and closed for just one hour to clean up. We were having a fabulous time.

The one thing that I always did was go to church on Sunday. I just had to go to church. It was driven into my head from when I was a small child to go to church every Sunday, and it never left me. I had to pray for the Colts because this was such a special game that they needed help to win. I got in the car and started to drive, and after asking a few people, I found the church. I attended Mass, and after the services were over, I went up to the altar to pray to the Blessed Mother, I lit a candle, and asked Her to please help the Colts. I told Her they needed Her help. I said to the Blessed Mother, "They have come such a long way, please don't let all of their efforts be in vain. Please, please help them." I believed that if you prayed hard enough for something, it would happen, and I have believed this all of my life.

Our Ride to the Super Bowl

When I returned to the hotel, to my surprise, there were buses across the street from the hotel, and there were also six cops on motorcycles. I went into our room and found Clara busily fixing her girlfriend's hair. I told her about the buses outside across the street from our hotel. I said to Clara, "I don't know how we are going to do this, but we are going to get on those buses to go to the stadium." I didn't know where I was going, and I didn't want to be stuck in all the traffic. I just thought it would be better to hitch a ride with someone instead of being unsure of where we were supposed to go and maybe even missing the game, the main reason we came to Florida in the first place, and I certainly didn't want to do that.

While I worked at Unitas', there were buses taking people to the stadium to attend the game all of the time, so I knew that these buses were also going to the stadium today. Where else would the buses be going on this special day? We went outside and stood across the street from the buses, and we held up the Johnny Unitas sign that Clara's friend had made for us. By then, the people started coming out of the hotel across the street from our hotel. When they saw the sign, and us, they said, "Come on, sweetheart; we'll give you a ride to the stadium." We went onto the buses to go to the Super Bowl, along with Clara's friend who still didn't have a ticket. The people asked us where we were from, and when they found out I worked at Unitas', they were enthusiastic and started to ask me a lot of questions about him. When they found out Clara's friend didn't have a ticket. They said, "Don't worry about a thing sweetheart; we will get you a ticket to the game." They saw three beautiful girls, and that was enough for them to be happy. They had booze and a band on the bus.

Oh, and the six cops on motor cycles gave us a police escort to the Super Bowl. The first three cops went up to the first street and stopped the traffic, while the next three cops went up to the second street and stopped the traffic there. This went on all the way to the stadium, and the entire time that we were on our way to the stadium, the motorcycle cops had their sirens blasting all the time. It was wild.

When we arrived at the stadium, one of the men from the buses bought Clara's friend a ticket, which he paid a scalper $100 for, a lot of money back then. The only stipulation was that the girl had to sit with this man during the game. There were 84,000 people at the game, and we thought it would be okay for her to sit with the man during the game. What could he do to her with all of these people around them?

All the sports writers said the game was going to be boring, but it was just the opposite. All through the game Clara's friend kept coming to where we were sitting and kept asking Clara to leave the game and go back to the hotel with her. After the third time she did this, the people who were sitting around us became annoyed. They kept telling us to sit down.

Finally, I said, "Clara, the only reason we came here was to see this game. If you leave with her, I am going to be very upset with you!" Clara told her friend that she wasn't going to leave the game.

I said, "Clara, what if he does see her, all she is doing is watching the game. There were all of those people there, what is she going to do? She isn't doing anything wrong." Because Clara would not leave with her, the girl finally left and took a cab back to the hotel. Clara and I stayed and watched the entire game, and what a game it was.

I was on the edge of my seat through the whole game. The Colts never gave up; they kept on persevering. The Colts retrieved three interceptions, which was one of the major reasons why the game was so exciting. The Dallas Cowboys were so rough that when they hit Johnny this one time, they broke Johnny U's ribs during the game right in front of where we were sitting. The impact on Johnny was so severe that you could hear Johnny's ribs crack all the way up on the thirty-yard line in the stand where we were sitting. Because of his injury, Johnny had to leave the game, and this is one of the reasons why the game was so close. If Johnny had finished the game, it might have been a different ending, but Earl Morrell had to come in to finish the game for him.

I believe Earl wanted to prove himself after the awful loss to the Jets a few years ago. Earl then went on to lead the Colts to the game winning Jim O'Brien field goal in the last three minutes of the game. Even though the Colts had the option to go into overtime, they placed everything on Jim O'Brien, who was the kicker for the Colts at this time. With a swift jerk of the knee, the Colts won.

It was a good thing that I had gone to church to pray for them. I'm positive the Blessed Mother helped them.

The Big Party

The people told us to meet them back at the buses and they would give us a ride back to the hotel. When we returned to the bus, the rest of the people also returned. We had no idea of what was about to happen. Remember the police on motorcycles? Well they were there for us again. We had a police escort back to the hotel. I was screaming I couldn't believe it. What a fantastic time we were having. It was a positively marvelous, fabulous event.

The people we were with were from a club from New York and New Jersey. They were called the "Touchdown Club," and at every Super Bowl, they did the same routine. Some people had bet on the Colts and some had bet on the Cowboys. Some people had won a lot of money, and others had lost a lot of money. But you would never have known it because they were all having a fabulous time. The people invited us to their hotel. They told us that there would be a huge buffet, and what a great feast we had. Clara and I ate and had a drink, and then we left, because I only had one more night left, and we still had a lot of Miami to explore. We tried to find out where the Colts were, but to no avail, it was all hush-hush. We couldn't find them, but this did not stop us from having a fantastic time anyway.

The Plane Ride Home

The next day, I had to take the plane home by myself because I had to go back to work. Clara and her friend could stay another day because they had a couple more days off. Clara took me to the airport and dropped me off under the assumption that I would be okay. I had to fly back to Baltimore alone.

When the plane took off, it made a funny noise.

I was sitting next to a complete stranger, and I said to her, "The plane did not make this noise when it took off."

She was very polite and tried to console me, and said, "Everything will be all right; it is just your imagination."

The pilot then came on the loud speaker and told us there was mechanical difficulty, and we would have to turn around and go back to the airport. I was a nervous wreck. We all had to leave the plane and go back into the airport. By then, Clara had already gone back to the hotel and I had no way of getting in touch with her.

I went to the phone booth and called Mom and Dad and started to cry. I told them I was sorry for not telling them where I was going. I was worried that I would never see the children again. I told them to please kiss them for me and tell them that I loved them. I was sure that I was being punished for not telling my parents where I was going. I was so frightened and all alone in the airport, I began to pray the rosary. Soon after this, the airline called us to return to the plane. My nerves were really acting up big time by now. I couldn't wait to come home to see the children and my parents. I prayed all the way home.

I picked up my children and hugged and kissed them as if there was no tomorrow. I promised them that I would never leave them again, and I haven't. I went to my parents' home, and they were glad to see me also. I was never scolded for what I had done because my parents were truly glad to see me home safe and sound.

On the news later that evening, I heard that the Colts were coming home. I took the children and told them we were going to see Johnny U and the Colts come home. There were huge crowds to welcome the Colts home at the airport, and I was fearful the children and I would get trampled. We were right up against the fence where they had a stand set up for the Colts to speak when they got off the airplane. The people were pushing us up against the fence so hard that we left and went into the airport to go home. I didn't want anything to happen to the children. Just then, down the escalator came Johnny U from the plane. The children flew over to him, as they always did. We had finally gotten to congratulate him in person. He hugged and kissed the children, and we took some pictures together. We went home and I finally went to sleep, something I desperately needed after my hectic weekend. What a wonderful experience. It was the best time I ever had in my whole life.

The Football

When I went back to work at the restaurant, I got a football from Johnny U and I got every one of the Colts players to sign it. Instead of keeping the football for my children, I gave it to my sister, because I thought that she and her husband would appreciate it, since her husband had nephews. They also had a house and seemed to have a more stable life than I had. I was afraid that I might lose it, and with something that valuable, I didn't want to chance it.

Years passed, and I always thought the football was in a "safe place." Little did I know that my sister and her husband were not sports nuts like me, and did not treasure the football. Rosie had a super bowl party one year and everyone from the family was there. During the game, I asked Rosie to bring out the football that I gave to her years ago.

My sister said, "What football, Peach?"

I said, "What football? You know the one with all the Colts players' autographs all over it."

Rosie then told me she gave the football to her friend to sell at a yard sale. "YARD SALE." "YARD SALE." "YARD SALE." The words were hanging in the air. I couldn't believe what I was hearing. How could she do such a thing with such a treasure?

By the time that I found out what she had done, it was too late to get the football back. I told her, "Do you know how much that football is worth today?" Many people had told me it would be worth thousands of dollars. She still could not comprehend the value of what I had given her. She could not understand why I was so upset.

Upper right: Peachy and Clara Tana on the way to Super Bowl V in Miami. Above: Peachy's boss Johnny Unitas—with Peachy's daughters Michelle and Anna—would suffer a game-ending rib injury in the second quarter of the championship game. Right: Anna, Rosie, Michelle, and Bernie at Easter.

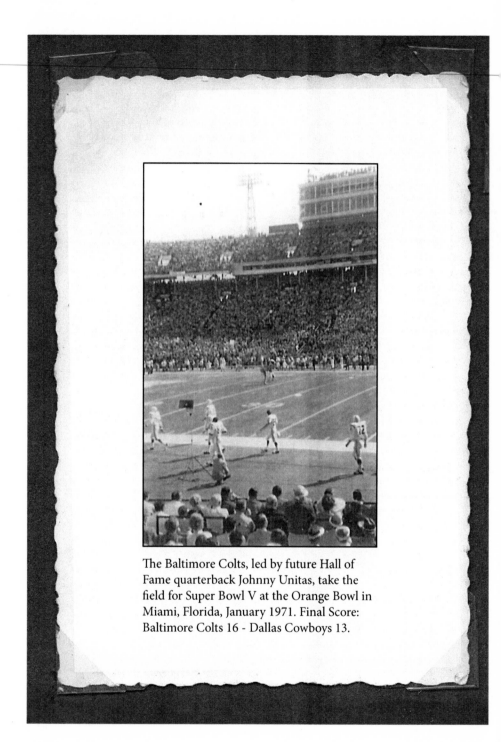

The Baltimore Colts, led by future Hall of
Fame quarterback Johnny Unitas, take the
field for Super Bowl V at the Orange Bowl in
Miami, Florida, January 1971. Final Score:
Baltimore Colts 16 - Dallas Cowboys 13.

Twenty: Haussner's

After working at Johnny U's for four-and-a-half years, I left and went to work at Haussner's Restaurant in Highlandtown. It was so close to my home that I could walk back and forth to work. It was a German restaurant with a huge menu, specializing in seafood such as broiled or stuffed lobster tails, stuffed shrimp, shrimp creole, salmon, and crab cakes. All of the food was cooked to order. They even had frog legs. They also had delicious German food such as sauerbraten, wiener schnitzel, bratwurst, sour beef and scrumptious dumplings, and many other German dishes. They had any kind of potato you could imagine, broccoli, spinach, stewed tomatoes, pickled beets, peas, cabbage, eggplant, and thirty-seven other vegetables. There were over a dozen homemade desserts such as strawberry pie (with huge strawberries), coconut custard pie, peach pie, cherry pie, strawberry shortcake, apple strudel, German chocolate cake, cheese cake, eclairs, and carrot cake.

There would be people lined up outside of the building and wrapped around the block every evening. Dad insisted that I go there and work because it was close to home and the restaurant was closed on Sunday. He said, "If the restaurant is closed on Sundays then you would be able to spend more time with the children, Mom and me, and then we could go somewhere together." I applied for the job, but they did not call me for almost a month. When they hired me, they put me in a training period, something that I wasn't prepared to do because I was taking care of the children by myself.

Another Restaurant Job

Let me explain what the inside of Haussner's looked like. It was a huge building that seated about five hundred people. Mr. and Mrs. Haussner traveled the world, and during their travels, they purchased paintings and statues that were valued over millions of dollars. It looked exactly like an art museum with a restaurant inside of it. The pictures and statues lined every aisle and covered every room. Each aisle had its own name, and the waitresses were assigned to different sections. One station was so far away from the kitchen that you would have to walk almost a city block to get to it. This was the only station I didn't care for.

There was a men only bar, because it had pictures of naked women lining the walls, and Mr. and Mrs. Haussner thought this would not be appropriate for women or children to look at. The basement was called the Rathskeller. This was where the people would wait to be seated if there was inclement weather. They also used it for parties of large amounts of people. In the early days, the Haussners held dances there.

Mr. Haussner got an idea to collect all of the string that the napkins were wrapped in. Every time a bundle of napkins was delivered, they would be tied in string. Mr. Haussner told his employees to gather all of the string from the napkins, which he rolled into a ball. Eventually the enormous ball was kept in the basement. People would come just to look at the ball of string and were amazed at its size.

At Christmas time, the Haussners had the room decorated with little moveable figurines that the Haussners purchased for the children to enjoy during the Christmas holidays. During the rest of the year, the upstairs would just display a large mural depicting the Civil War between the north and the south. It was only a small section of a battle scene that was originally as huge as a football field. Mr. and Mrs. Haussner had bought the small section at an auction for their restaurant. Eventually the upstairs would only be used for banquets.

The gigantic kitchen had different sections where the waitresses had to go to pick up the food. Everything was made fresh in house every day.

The bar was on the right side of the kitchen, which is where we went to pick up drinks for the customers. To the left of the bar were bins that held all of the freshly baked muffins and bread. We would get a basket of bread together to serve to the customers. The chocolate muffins were my favorite, but they also had blueberry and cherry muffins. I gained so much weight while I worked at Haussner's, primarily because of the chocolate muffins.

To the right of the bread bins was the area were we ordered and picked up the seafood dishes, which were baked or broiled. They cooked everything to order, and therefore it took a long time to pick up the food. Because of this, the waitresses spent the majority of their time in the kitchen trying to pick up their food. To the left of that area we ordered and picked up all of the meat dishes, which were also cooked to order. The cooks on the meat side cooked steaks, rabbit, tongue, sour beef and dumplings, and all kinds of dishes that I had never heard of before. Mom only cooked Italian dishes, and while I worked at Haussner's I found this completely new assortment of food.

In front of the meat dishes was a large section that held the forty-five vegetables. In the back of that, there was a little lady who cooked eggplant, onion rings, and French fries to order. Next to the vegetable sections were the soups and salads and various kinds of dressings. During the day, employees, who were ladies from the neighborhood, would cut up all of the vegetables for the salads. Mrs. Haussner was a vegetarian, and the ladies would make her a juice extract from all of the vegetables. She drank a combination of vegetable juice every day, and perhaps this is why she had the most wonderful complexion. Next to the vegetables, a male cook would fry all of the seafood such as crab cakes, shrimp, and mixed seafood platters. Behind this was the bakery, where bakers would prepare all of the famous strawberry pies, cakes, breads, and muffins. Oh, the smells that came from the kitchen were just fabulous.

In the back of the kitchen were many older neighborhood women, who were employed as dishwashers. They always made sure the silver, glasses, and dishes were spotless. Little ladies with carts would roam the dining room to clear the tables and prepare them for the next seating. Even though they were elderly, they sure could move fast.

At the entrance stood many hostesses who greeted the customers and took them to their tables. Because there were so many rooms they needed many hostesses. Some of the hostesses were attractive, but many of them were just ordinary people who also lived in the neighborhood.

As the customers entered the restaurant, they would pass by the most delicious display of desserts imaginable. The elderly ladies of the neighborhood also worked the pie case, which displayed the famous strawberry pies.

Most of the employees at Haussner's had worked there for many years, and most of them lived on the east side of town near the restaurant. The employees could walk back and forth to work, and I believe this is the reason they worked there for such a long time.

The Card Store

There was a greeting card store up the street from Haussner's. The waitresses who worked the split shift would go there on their break, just to get out of the restaurant for a little while. One of the girls bought a special pin and came back to work wearing it on her uniform. The ladies behind the counter who sold all the desserts saw the pretty design on the pin and liked it so much that they said to the waitress, "Where did you get the beautiful pin?"

The girl said, "Oh, you like the pin, I'll get you one." The waitress went back to the card store and bought a pin for each of the ladies behind the pie case. Guess what the pin was? It was a pin shaped into a marijuana leaf.

All the elderly ladies who worked behind the pie case wore the pin and were proud of it. When customers commented on the pin, the ladies would say, "Oh, you like this pin, one of the waitresses got it for us."

Each waitress at Haussner's only had three tables to work at a time. Sometimes customers at one of the tables wanted to sit and talk among themselves, and that meant that you only had two tables left to work with. It was hard to make a living there. When I worked at other restaurants, I always had about four or five tables at a time. With only three tables, it was difficult to earn enough to meet my commitments. Most of the girls were married and used the income that they made at the restaurant to supplement the household. It didn't matter to them whether they were busy or not. I, on the other hand, was always robbing Peter to pay Paul.

Haussner's was an established business, and it closed early every night and was closed on Sunday and Monday. The managers made the schedule according to seniority. When I started there, I had to prove that I was a qualified waitress before I was put on the split shift. When I finally was put on the split shift, I was so excited because I thought that I was finally going to be able to make sufficient money to provide for my family. As we left the kitchen with the food, there would be a manager standing there, supervising us to make sure the food was hot and looked presentable to serve to the customers. After I had worked the split shift for a couple of days, the manager told me that he wanted to talk to me about something. Oh my goodness, I thought that I had done something wrong. I was a nervous wreck. I went to the manager to ask him what he wanted me for, and he told me, "You have to wear a girdle, because you wiggle too much when you walk."

The Many Curves in the Restaurant

Trying to pick up the food from the kitchen was extremely difficult. Everywhere we went to pick up the food, we would have to wait in line. There were thirty-three waitresses working at one time. We could pick up our own soups and salads, but as far as everything else, we had to wait for the cooks to give us our order. This was also the only restaurant that I worked that did not have a dupe system. All we did was call out our orders, and the cooks were supposed to remember who ordered what food. By the time we got the food, we had left our customers alone in the dining room for a long time.

There was one little lady at Haussner's who had worked there forever, and she was up in age, but that didn't stop her from working. She would often strike me in the back of my ankles with her cart. She would say, "Watch your shape, young lady," which meant get out of my way I'm coming through. I would have torn panty hose or bruised ankles by the end of every Saturday evening.

Only a few girls who worked at the restaurant were single like me. We became friends because we were in the same circumstances taking care of our children by ourselves. One of the girls, named Marge, had two teenage children who would watch my children in the evening for me. My parents watched them for me in the daytime, but they needed a break in the evening. Since Marge's children, Sherrie and Bobbie, were young, they could relate to Anna and Michelle. The children really had a great time while they were in the company of Sherrie and Bobby because they spent quality time playing with them.

There was a little pub across the street from the restaurant, and many of the waitresses and bartenders would go there after work to have a drink and unwind. The owners of the Irish pub were friendly and they welcomed all the business from the waitresses and bartenders. It was a small place, nothing fancy, but it was homey. The owner, Ray, was so personable, always with a smile on his face and a joke to tell. He was so warm and friendly that even today we are still friends.

There was a wonderful boy that I met while working at Haussner's. He worked very hard carrying everything that was needed up and down the basement steps. He was like my girlfriend because he would call me everyday asking me how I was. I even brought him with me to Sabatino's when I went there to work, although I was afraid of how they would treat him because he was gay. But don't you know that all those macho men at Sabatino's just loved him. His name is Bobby, and this friendship has lasted up until today.

Mom and Dad Watching the Children

As the years passed, I remained close to my parents. I always stayed in Highlandtown, even when all of my girlfriends had moved to Towson. I always wanted to be near my parents. I needed them in my life for support and comfort. Every Saturday, Dad would take the children for a walk after breakfast. The walk consisted of doing all of his chores, and while he did this he would bring the children with him, and they really thought they were going somewhere. While they were out, Mom could get her housework done.

First, they would go to the camera store to pick up pictures from last week and drop off more film from this past week. (While the children were young, we would take lots of pictures of them.) Then they would stop at the post office to purchase stamps and to mail letters. Their next stop was the library to return the books and to pick up more books for the coming week. Then they went to the bank where Dad would put one dollar in each of their accounts every week. His next stop was Woolworth's five-and-dime store to pick up whatever Mom needed for the house. After that, he stopped at Hoehn's bakery to pick up donuts and cheesecake so that there would be special treats for us on Sunday after church. The next to the last stop was Diamond's cleaners to pick up the clean clothes to wear to church on Sunday. Their final stop would be to the chicken store to buy fresh chicken and eggs for Mom.

When they finally came home, they would eat lunch, and Mom would put a huge blanket on the living room floor for the girls to take a nap. When they woke up they would watch wrestling with Dad, and Mom would make her famous chili to go with hot dogs, this was their Saturday night treat from Mom.

Mom's Famous Chili Recipe

She would ask Dad to go to the store with the children and buy fresh beef cubes. She would then have the butcher grind the beef twice to make sure it would be tender. Then, in a medium pot, she would place the ground beef, onions, salt and pepper and a large can of tomato puree all together. She would then let the ingredients cook for a couple hours. She would stir it often so it would not burn.

It was just wonderful, as was everything she cooked for us.

The children would have to dice the onions in the chopper for the hot dogs. Daddy bought a hand slicer which he thought was a wonderful invention. He used the slicer to cut potatoes, and he would say, "Phil, look at this. We can make our own French fries." He thought this was simply marvelous. After Saturday's dinner, they would have to grate the Parmesan cheese, which they bought from DiPasquale's grocery store, for our Sunday spaghetti and meatballs dinner. He would involve the children in everything that Mom and he did.

When the children got older, Dad taught them how to play checkers and five-hundred rummy. He even made his own checkerboard. He painted it, and the board looked exactly like a real checkerboard. They would play games all day long, and the children loved him because he spent prime time with them. Dad would play these games with the children during the hot summer because it didn't take much energy. My parents did not have an air conditioner, so they had to keep the children amused and comfortable despite the heat.

Going to Vincent's

During the summer, I often took the girls to Vince's house, because he had a swimming pool in his back yard. On Sunday, Mom and Dad would come over to Vince's also and we would have a big picnic in his back yard. Dad told Vince how lucky he was to have a sister who came over his house and cleaned and cooked for him. Vince had been divorced for a number of years, and he only had a limited amount of resources. He was extremely upset over his divorce, and I tried to lift him up by filling his life with the children and me.

While I worked at Haussner's, I took the children to Vince's and we would spend a whole week there at a time. Funds were low at this time in my life so I toke the children to Vince's instead of going to Ocean City. We had so much fun at Vince's swimming in his pool all day, cleaning his house for him, and cooking nice dinners for him to eat when he came home from work.

In the evening, I would take the children to the movies, or sometimes Vince would take us to BWI airport to watch the planes take off and land. He lived right near the airport, and he made this another special treat for the children and me. We were amused just watching the planes take off and land. There was no security like there is now so you could get close to watch the planes and no one said anything to us.

Someone had constructed a huge slide in Glen Burnie on Ritchie Highway. When you slid down the slide, you would land in sand. It gave you the feeling of being at the beach, and the children just thought it was wonderful, and they would say, "Again mommy, again please." So up the steps we would go to slide down the giant slide again and again and the children thought that we had a wonderful vacation. They just loved having me spend quality time with them.

When I went back to work, the girls I worked with asked me, "Where did you go on your vacation, Leonora?

I replied, "I went to Glen Burnie." They all laughed.

During the winter months Vince would take the girls ice-skating and roller-skating. The children just loved all the attention he gave them. On skating days, the children would wait by the window for Vince to come and pick them up, and when he pulled up in front of Mom and Dad's house they would scream, "He's here, he's here!"

Going to the Ocean

One summer, I wanted my parents to come to Ocean City with us, but for some unknown reason, which I still haven't figured out, Dad was always afraid to leave the house for long periods of time. He worried that something would happen to our house. I was annoyed that I had lost one day of my vacation waiting for my parents to make up their minds if they were coming to the ocean with me and the children so I left without them.

The very next day they followed me right down to the ocean. Rosie also came to the ocean with her girlfriends. Most of the family was there, so my parents really felt as though they had to come also.

I had rented an apartment that did not have an air conditioner, but I didn't mind because it was in my price range. When my parents arrived, they wanted me to leave my apartment immediately and come and stay with them. Naturally, I did because the apartment that I had rented was stifling. Besides, I always listened to my parents. We all spent our days on the beach and our nights on the boardwalk taking the children on the rides, and we had another wonderful time together. This was truly a vacation for Mom this time, because she didn't have to cook or do laundry or any of the household chores that she would have to do if she were home.

One August day, when we were leaving the beach, I turned the radio on in the car. There was a news flash that said Elvis Presley had died. The announcer said that he thought that this was a prank, but to stay tuned for further information. They were investigating these rumors. I rushed back to our room so I could turn on the television to watch the news. Our favorite news anchorman, Jerry Turner on Channel 13, was on, and what he reported was not good. He told us that it was not a rumor at all and that the early reports were true. I was glued to the TV set. I could not believe what the reports were saying about Elvis. They told us he had been taking heavy drugs for some time, all of which were prescription, and they believed that this was the reason that he had died. He had used certain drugs to go to sleep and used other drugs to wake up. I didn't want to believe it. He was a person who always appeared to be in control of his life. How could this awful thing happen to him? I was heartbroken. He had been my idol all of my life. I had been following his career ever since I was a teenager. I was devastated.

The Big Picnic

During the summer, a politician friend of Uncle Mimi's had an end of the summer picnic at his farm. He told Uncle Mimi that he could invite his family, and so he did, because he liked being with his family also. Because summer was ending, the politician friend of Uncle Mimi's wanted to give everyone some of his corn because he had such an abundance of it. Dad, you may remember, was not clear with directions, and the farm was on the Maryland–Pennsylvania line. He felt the need to take a trial run since he always got lost as soon as he left Highlandtown. One day he asked my brother to take a ride with him. He said, "Johnny come and help me find the farm so I won't get lost on the day we go on the picnic."

They found the farm just fine, and I'm sure it was because Johnny went. On the way home, there was a fruit stand on the side of the road. Dad wanted to stop and get some fresh fruit and vegetables to bring home to Mom. There was a pretty girl who worked the fruit stand, and Dad said to Johnny, "Look at the pretty girl Johnny, why don't you ask her out?" Little did Dad know that Johnny was already dating another woman. In fact, she was the woman who owned the corner store right down the street from our home. Johnny already had stability at home with Mom. He wanted someone to make him laugh. He was looking for someone to have fun with. After being with Mom, who did everything for him throughout his entire life, he wanted something else. Johnny had fallen for the storeowner. She was beautiful and witty, and Johnny loved her very much.

Johnny's Tragedy

Years later, Johnny married the lady from the corner store. Her name was Arta. They were married for several years, and she made Johnny very happy. She was an excellent cook and she always kept Johnny in stitches because of her quick wit.

Many years passed and one night I got a call from Arta, that Johnny had a heart attack and was in the hospital. She told me that Johnny did not feel good by noon, and she had to force him to get in the ambulance to go to the hospital. Even though she got him to the hospital in the early afternoon, she did not call me until 8:30 in the evening. Johnny was in the hospital all day, just lying there. The hospital had no facilities to help someone if they had a heart attack. If I were there earlier, I would have insisted that they move him to another hospital that could have opened up his closed artery.

After I arrived at the hospital, I started screaming "Johnny, Johnny, Johnny get up! Come on, Johnny, get up get out of the bed." After I created a scene, the doctors decided to move him to another hospital that had the equipment to open up his artery. The only thing wrong with this was that it was all the way on the other side of town. The whole family drove there, Vince and Grace, Rosie and Bernie, me and Aunt Lena, Arta and her son. We were all in the waiting room together. Suddenly the doctor came out to talk to us.

He said, "Who is with Mr. DiPietro?"

We all answered, "We are."

The doctor was shocked to see so many people in the hospital for one person at this time of night. Soon after he went back into the hospital to work on my brother, he came back and told us that Johnny had passed. Everyone in the room was hysterical. How could this wonderful strong, healthy looking person die so suddenly?

Later, I found out the reason why. Johnny's job was so stressful. His company would send him all over the country to collect money that was owed to them. Johnny also smoked heavily, and ate lots of salty food. With all these obstacles against him, he didn't have a chance. My poor brother was gone.

The one thing that I cannot get out of my mind is that I could have saved him, and I didn't. Once when I was talking to Johnny, he told me he didn't feel good. I thought that he just had indigestion, and that he would be okay. I didn't think he was that sick. I didn't know all the stress that Johnny had in his life. If I had paid more attention to him, I would have made him go to a doctor to get a check-up. Johnny was younger than I, and he was always so much stronger than me. I just never thought anything would happen to him. Why oh why didn't I insist that he go and get a check-up? Why didn't I do more to help him? I could have saved him from his demise and I didn't. I will have to live with the guilt that I could have saved my brother's life forever, and the pain will be with me all the days of my life.

The Day of the Picnic

The day of the picnic finally arrived. Dad told me to make sure that I was at the house early so we could pack the car with all of the goodies that Mom made to take to the picnic. Aunt Lena brought her homemade pasta, meat balls, and sauce, and Mom brought her fried chicken and potato salad. And even though dad had practiced the route to the farm, he still had to follow Aunt Lena and Uncle Fritz so he would not get lost.

We were halfway to the picnic, when all of a sudden Dad said, "Oh hell, Phil, I left my teeth home." At that point, I lost it. I was laughing so hard that I almost wet myself. I could not stop laughing. After all of the preparation, Dad had forgotten his own amenities – his teeth.

After containing myself from all of the laughter, I said "Dad, after we get to the picnic, I will go back home with you to get your teeth." But after we got to the picnic, he did not want to leave because his entire family was there. He stayed there all day, ate the food, and gummed the corn without his teeth. His gums were sore for several weeks after the festival. Poor Dad, he was such a good person. He was in terrible pain, but he never complained about anything.

Dad was the main character in my life, the one person who always tried to lead me down the right path. He would always try to point me in the right direction so that I was able to take care of myself in case anything happened to him. One of the things that Dad drove into my head was that I had to leave something for my children. I would say, "Dad how can I do this, I hardly have enough money to pay my bills now? There never is anything left over." He would insist that I try, because this was what he was always taught by his parents, Save, save, save. You never know when your rainy day is coming.

Top left: Phyllis and Carmen DiPietro with granddaughters Anna and Michelle at Ocean City, Maryland, July 1969. Top right: Peachy working at Haussner's, the famous Baltimore restaurant at Eastern Avenue and Clinton Street. Above: Aunts and uncles at the corn festival include Aunt Lena, Aunt Mary, Uncle Charlie, Uncle Fritz, and Uncle Alex, August 1971.

Twenty-One: Sabatino's

After Clara and I returned from Florida, we would make it a point to take our children out every Friday evening. We wanted to compensate for our absence in their lives. When I got off on Friday afternoon, I would pick up Anna and Michelle from my parents' home, and then I would go to Clara's beauty shop, "Jolie Danielle," and wait for her to finish work. Then we would pick up Danielle, Clara's daughter, and we would all go out to dinner together.

We'd take all the girls to our favorite restaurant in Little Italy, Sabatino's. Clara's friend, Mulkie, worked there as the barmaid and got her hair done at Jolie Danielle every week. Mulkie was a middle aged woman with brown eyes and brown hair. She had lost her teeth, but that didn't matter because she had the best personality. She would tell us all these stories about the different things that happened in Little Italy, and because they were so funny she would always make us laugh. She talked about Sabatino's all the time and told us they had the best food in Little Italy.

While Mulkie worked at Sabatino's, she was always joking with the customers and then she would say a cuss word and the customers would burst out laughing. The customers loved to hear her say those nasty words. Everyone felt that they had to be prim and proper, but she would help them let their hair down.

Mulkie told the people that she worked with that Clara and I would be coming to Sabatino's, and because of this the people treated us special. The Maitre d' at Sabatino's at this time was an extraordinary person, with a fabulous personality, named Mustard, who treated our children, Clara, and I wonderfully. He was a forty-year-old man, short and stocky with brown hair and brown eyes, and always had a huge smile for everyone. He was especially kind to our children. Mustard would put each of my girls on his knees and tell them, "You kids can eat whatever you want. I don't care what your mother says. If you want lobster, you can have lobster. Just order whatever you want." And as much as they came to love him, the only treat they really wanted was a Shirley Temple with extra cherries! The children, Clara, and I spent many Friday evenings at Sabatino's. This was the beginning of a relationship that lasted for many years.

Mustard was always trying to get me to come to work for Sabatino's. He said if I came to work there I could make good tips. I just couldn't comprehend working until three o'clock in the morning. I had a problem digesting this, and besides whom could I get to watch the children all that time? My parents needed a break, and I didn't want to leave them with just anyone. I didn't want to wake up in the morning and not have the children with me. I worked so many hours that I wanted to have breakfast with them before they went to school. They would be gone all day at school, and by the time they would come home, I would be getting ready to go to work. This is the main reason why I didn't want to work so late at night.

When I worked at Haussner's, on the weekends, the restaurant closed between ten and eleven o'clock at night. It never stayed open late. I would take the children out to eat after work, sometimes at Bud's crab house. People would look at me as if to say why are you bringing the children out so late at night? They could not realize how much I missed my children. I wanted to spend as much time as possible with them, even if it meant late in the evening, when I got off of work.

The New Beginning

Finally, after working for three and a half years at Haussner's, and not being able to have money left over to have a good time with my children, I made the decision to call my friend Mulkie and ask her if it would be possible for me to get a job at Sabatino's. Mulkie arranged for me to come in and talk to the owner's nephew, Vince, because he was the person who did all the hiring. When I told him I worked at Haussner's, he hired me immediately. I was amazed because there was no training period. I didn't have to follow anyone and I was able to pick up tables right after I was hired. There was no working just a half of a shift, I was put on the floor immediately, which was hard considering I had to learn their new system with all the different food they served.

Sabatino's was the busiest restaurant in Little Italy, mainly because of the wonderful food that the owner-chef, Joe Canzani would prepare for his customers. Everyone would come in to see him, because they knew that when he was cooking in the kitchen, everything came out perfect. The customers would even comment that they knew Joe was cooking in the kitchen, because the parsley was placed just so on their dishes.

One Saturday evening I was waiting on a table of six people right in front of the bar, where all the managers were standing. I was carrying a tray of food out of the kitchen. After I put the tray down, I went to serve the food to the customers, all of a sudden I dropped a Veal Francese with the white wine sauce down the customer's back, while all the managers were standing right there. I thought I was going to be fired for sure. I apologized several times to the customer and offered to have his jacket cleaned and to my surprise not one of my bosses said a word to me, and the customer was not upset. I couldn't believe it. What a miracle.

Every Saturday evening, it was very busy. There would be a line outside the door and down the block. Ricky, Vince, Albert, and Baron would be seating the people and they would keep telling us to drop the check, drop the check, because they needed to seat more customers.

On one Saturday evening, Joe became overwhelmed with all the orders he had to cook. He walked out of the restaurant and went out on the sidewalk to smoke a cigarette. He needed a break from all the checks that were coming into the kitchen. Vince went around to all the waitresses and had to collect all their orders, himself. Joe did not want any more checks to come in the kitchen until he finished cooking all the orders that were lined up all the way down the end of the line. He was such a perfectionist that if he couldn't make the dishes right, he didn't want to make them at all.

The restaurant was open every evening until three o'clock. After the dinner hour was over, we would have a little break until the theater let out around 10:30, and then the customers who attended the show would come in for a late night snack. Many celebrities would come into the restaurant after they performed at different places in

Baltimore, because Sabatino's was the only place open late at night to get a fine dinner.

The restaurant would also have the late night crowd after the bars closed. Around 1:30 A.M., a line would form out the door again. The people that came into the restaurant at this time came from all over Baltimore. They would be bar owners, and other people who worked in restaurants and bars. We would also get lots of people who had a little too much to drink. There were many nights that people would fall asleep in their food. A customer would be eating his spaghetti and meatballs, and all of a sudden his face would fall right in the bowl of spaghetti. Then the managers would have to go over to the customer and wake him up. It was a wild and crazy time then.

These things would only happen during the weekends, because during the week, unless something was happening downtown, we would not be busy. During this time of the week, all the locals from the neighborhood would came in for coffee and sat around until three o'clock talking to us and telling us all their funny stories. The stories were so hilarious, they were almost impossible to believe. This would keep us in stitches laughing, and before we knew it, it would be three o'clock, time to leave and go home. Because of the wonderful neighborhood people, the other waitresses and I felt safe walking the streets of Little Italy at three o'clock in the morning.

Waiting on Politicians

When it was election time in Baltimore, after the polls closed, all the local politicians would come into the restaurant. On this one memorable evening, while Jerry Brown was running for President, he came to Baltimore to try to convince the people of Baltimore to vote for him. All of a sudden, the restaurant became packed with all the local politicians, such as Governor Marvin Mandel, Mayor Tommy D'Alesandro, and all of the local politicians and dignitaries. Because Jerry Brown was a presidential candidate, the secret service men guarded the front door.

Tuesday evening was the only evening that Joe the owner would go home early. After all the people came in and the restaurant became packed, Vince called Joe and asked him to come back to the restaurant, because Jerry Brown was there. Joe asked, "Who is Jerry Brown?" and Vince said, "He just might be the next President of the United States." Joe came back to work, but he could not get into his restaurant. By now the secret service men were guarding the door, and because Joe always carried a gun for protection, they wouldn't let him in. Joe was at the front door calling, "Vincie, Vincie, they won't let me in my own restaurant!" Vince had to go over to the secret service men and explain to them who Joe was. Vince said, "You have to let him in, because he is the owner and chef, and he is the person who is going to cook the food for Jerry Brown." This was one of the most unforgettable evenings at Sabatino's. We were so busy, that we didn't get out of work until four o'clock in the morning.

The Movie Star

There was another evening while I was working in the upstairs dining room when Ricky, the manager, came upstairs and was looking around. He kept rubbing his chin and looking around at the people who were sitting at the tables. After he did this, he went back downstairs. A few minutes later he came back upstairs again and did the same thing. After the third time, I asked him what he needed. He told me not to say anything to anyone, but that Al Pacino was coming into the restaurant and didn't want to be bothered by anyone. Ricky told me that the night before, Al Pacino was in Fells Point and he had gotten mobbed by people. Ricky told me that the people had torn Pacino's clothes off of him, and he needed a police escort to get out of Fells Point. He said that Pacino had just finished filming *And Justice For All*, and he just wanted to have a nice dinner and relax and not be bothered. So when my younger, very beautiful friend Kathy and I waited on Pacino, we were a pair of cool cucumbers. We waited on him as if he was a regular person. This was another fabulous evening at Sabatino's.

A Special Visitor

There was the time when President Carter was campaigning in

Little Italy. Mayor Tommy D'Alesandro lived in Little Italy and he would bring all the famous politicians there, along with my Uncle Mimi. President Carter did not eat at Sabatino's, Instead, he ate across the street at our "rival" restaurant, Chiapparelli's. There was one photographer who was not allowed into Chiapparelli's because all the secret service men would not let him in. He was carrying all of this heavy photography equipment, and he asked Vince, my boss, if he could come into Sabatino's to eat and Vince said sure, and fed him for free. When the photographer was finished eating, he asked Vince if he read the *Washington Post*, and Vince told him that he didn't. The photographer told him to get it tomorrow because there would be something in it that he would like.

When President Carter was leaving Chipparelli's with his entourage of secret service men and local politicians, this particular photographer took a picture of President Carter walking the streets of Little Italy. Behind the picture of President Carter was the sign for Sabatino's restaurant. The caption read only that President Carter had lunch in Little Italy in Baltimore. Thus, it appeared as though President Carter ate at Sabatino's instead of Chipparelli's. Mr. Chiapparelli called my boss Vince and said, "You know that President Carter ate at my restaurant, but the picture makes him look like he ate at your restaurant." Mr. Chiapparelli was very upset, but Vince just laughed.

While President Carter was in Baltimore, Uncle Mimi took him to visit Highlandtown, and there were also many pictures taken there of them.

Another famous politician who visited Sabatino's was Senator Ted Kennedy. Oddly enough, he was campaigning against Jimmy Carter. Although I did not have the pleasure of waiting on him, I felt especially honored to have seen him in person. He was a very quiet and reserved man while he was in the restaurant. This was another memorable day at Sabatino's.

The New Dishes

There was a judge who would frequent the restaurant, his name was Judge Robinson, and the owner created a dish especially for him, it is called Veal Jerome. The veal is dipped in an egg and cheese batter and then sautéed and served dry with lemon. The judge would come into the restaurant every Friday evening with a young district attorney, who is now also a judge, Judge Murphy.

Renato, who now is one of the owners of Sabatino's, also created a dish for his little son Renato when he was born, called Shrimp Renato. The shrimp is sautéed in a light brandy, lemon and butter sauce and served with melted cheese and prosciutto ham on top.

I can tell you first hand that both dishes are delicious.

The Bookmaker Salad

Another Maitre d' who worked at Sabatino's was Al. Al had many friends who would patronize the restaurant, and when they came in, he would go back in the kitchen and make his special salad for them. He called it the Bookmaker Salad for obvious reasons. The salad consisted of lettuce, tomatoes, onions, cheese, salami, shrimp, and egg with Sabatino's special house dressing. All of Al's friends would sit in the bar room, when the other customers walked by and saw this delicious looking salad, they would ask, "What is that?" Al replied, "It's the Bookmaker Salad."

During the day all the local judges and district attorneys would patronize Sabatino's along with all the local bookies. This group of people became the regular customers for lunch, and they soon became friends. The bookies and the judges and the district attorneys would all talk to each other even though they sat in different rooms. When Al made his special salad for all of his bookie friends, the judges and district attorneys saw it and they wanted it also. This is why the salad became so popular that the owners had to put it on the menu.

The Celebrities

Many celebrities have eaten at Sabatino's over the years as well: Tom Selleck, Billy Joel, Yul Brynner, Jerry Lewis, Bob Hope, Debbie Reynolds, Stevie Wonder, Mel Brooks, Bill Murray, Eddie Murphy, Will Smith, Ted Neely, and Barry Levinson, the Baltimore man who became the famous director of TV and films. Allan Charles, a partner at TBC advertising firm, and his son Josh Charles, the famous movie and TV star, have also dined at Sabatino's.

The Local Celebrities

There are also many prominent local families who have frequented Sabatino's, and here are some of them: the Millers (Sharon Miller helped me to edit my book several times); the Helmans (who own the largest carpet company in Baltimore, Bill's Carpet Fair) always bring their whole family; the Hirshfelds, owners of a store that sells sports apparel; the Bronsteins, owners of the Winner Distributing Company; Jerry and Sally Trout, prominent Baltimore realators; famous electronics retailer Jack Luskins, who made his name as "the cheapest guy in town," and his fmaily; the Balachous, a large family that gave me some very good information for my book; the Pozaneks also provided me with information; the Attmans, who own the Acme Paper Company; the Levinsons, who operate funeral homes; the Narons, who owned the Mary Sue candy company famous for its Easter Eggs; the Nusinovs, owners of a large jewelry company in Baltimore; the Hammermans have been friends with the owners of the restaurant for years; Carol and Stanley Alpert, Baltimore attorneys; the Getlans, another local lawyer and his family; the Ellises, a very friendly family; and the Franks, owners of the largest bail bonds business in Baltimore. Because these and so many other diners were all repeat customers, they developed a close relationship with the owners and me.

All the local TV personalities from Channels 13, 11, and 2 also dine at Sabatino's, as do all the local radio station personalities. There were also many sports figures that frequented the restaurant, as did the owners of sports teams like Steve Bisciotti (who owns the Ravens) and Peter Angelos (who owns the Orioles) as well as many of the well-known announcers. Over the years, Sabatino's became *the* spot to meet your favorite personalities while you were dining, and this is one of the reasons why the restaurant is so popular. That, and the delicious Italian food!

Special Visitor to Sabatino's

Perhaps my best night ever working at Sabatino's was the night that Frank Sinatra came there. Frank was appearing at The Merriweather Post Pavilion, in Columbia, Maryland, he called the restaurant to let them know he was coming there after the show. When the owners found out that Frank was coming to the restaurant they had the whole upstairs dining room remodeled in one day. I was walking up the street to come to work, when I saw workers throwing debris out of the upstairs fire escape. When I came into the restaurant, I asked some of the girls what was going on, but everyone was saying they didn't know. By five o'clock, they were installing new carpet on the steps leading to the upstairs dining room. They were nailing the carpet down the stairs, right while customers were having dinner in the restaurant.

Joe, the owner, was dressed in a cream colored shirt and matching pants. He always dressed impeccably. On this evening, while he was cooking, tomato sauce splashed on his shirt. He tried to get to stain off, but to no avail. He eventually had to borrow a shirt from Mulkie's husband Frank to wear.

Joe, with his protégée Renato, made special dishes for Frank Sinatra to enjoy while he was dining in the restaurant. After the dinner was over, and Frank was getting ready to leave, he looked at me and smiled. His eyes were as blue as the sky. This made my whole evening. All the older ladies from the neighborhood were outside waiting for him to leave, and don't you know that he hugged and kissed them all. There was a sub shop across the street from Sabatino's that had a jukebox that played all of Frank Sinatra's songs on it. The door was wide open and his music spilled out into the street. Frank had a fabulous time on this one night that he came to visit Sabatino's, and this started a custom that whenever Frank appeared in Baltimore, he would either come in or get take out.

Oprah and Renato

One time while Oprah had a show in Baltimore called *People Are Talking* with Richard Sher on Channel 13 in the morning, she had

Renato come on the show to cook the famous Veal Francese. Renato appeared in all his glamour wearing his gold chains, and prepared the dish for Oprah. While he was making the dish, Oprah kept asking him to explain all the ingredients that went into it. After the third time she asked him this question, Renato became upset and said, "How many times do you want me to say this?" He did not understand that she was trying to get the people at home to write the recipe down. We were watching this unfold on TV, and we burst out laughing because we all knew how excitable he would get when he was under pressure.

The Card Reader

There used to be a young girl who came to Sabatino's who would read cards. I became friendly with her, and I asked her to come back to the restaurant one Sunday evening. Normally it was not busy late Sunday nights, and I told her that she could read my cards then. When my bosses Joe and Ricky found out what she did, they insisted that she read their cards first. At the end of everyone's reading, she told all of us that a man in uniform was coming to visit us. None of us knew anyone in the service, and we couldn't understand why she told us this.

Earlier this evening the Baron, who was Joe's brother asked Joe to lend him some money so he could get into the poker game that was taking place across the street from Sabatino's. Joe lent Baron the money to get into the poker game. A few hours passed by when all of a sudden all the old men who were in the poker game, came running out of the building. The riot squad with their guns on their shoulders had climbed the walls of the building across the street from Sabatino's and raided the poker game. The police treated all the poker players like they were hardened criminals, when all along they were just a bunch of old men playing poker. While the police were putting all the old men into the paddy wagon, one of the old men gave Ricky his money to hold because he didn't want anything to happen to it. As the police were cuffing the man, Ricky gave the man shots of whiskey because he told the police he was having a heart attack. We saw all of this through the window, and Ricky filled us in on the rest when he came bursting in through the door. Just then we realized what the card reader was trying to tell us. The man in a uniform that was coming to see us at Sabatino's was the policeman.

My Friends

After working at Sabatino's for a while, I persuaded my friends Rita and Marge to join me. I told them even though you had to work until three o'clock in the morning, they would love it because they could make enough money to pay their bills. After many weeks of encouraging my friends to come to Sabatino's, they finally believed me and came to work there. They were happy, and so was I because I had my friends close by. This was the beginning of a long relationship that we all have had with Sabatino's for years.

Angie was a very loyal employee who worked for Sabatino's for forty-nine years. Angie watched out for everyone, her children, grandchildren, all the waitresses, busboys, bartenders, cooks, and customers, everyone but herself. If we ever had a problem, we would go to Angie, and she would help us solve it. The customers all loved her. Even though she gave them a hard time, she remembered what they liked to drink and eat. She would often have their drink waiting for them at their table. But sad to say, even though Angie took care of everyone, she neglected to take care of herself. Angie passed away on November 15, 2010, from a heart attack, leaving everyone of her friends and family wondering why she neglected herself so. Angie was there for such a long time, and she was a dear friend to me.

Top: DiPietro family gathers outside 3510 Claremont Street in the summer in the early '70s. (L-R) Peachy, Michelle, Bernie, Phyllis, Anna, Johnny, and Carmen (sitting). Middle: Rosie, Phyllis, and Peachy at Rosie's shower, 1974. Left: Bernie, Brian, and Rosie, 1974. Above: Carmen and Phyllis share a kiss.

Twenty-Two: Last Days of My Love

*E*very Friday evening, Rosie and Bernie went to Mom and Dad's after work, and I would meet them there. Rosie worked hard and long hours at a beauty shop in Highlandtown. When she came to Mom and Dad's, she could relax. Mom and Dad would also watch the children for me on Fridays, so I had to go there to pick up the children. We would have a small gathering every Friday evening around the kitchen table over Mom's coffee. Dad would be outside sitting on his rocking chair catching the breeze coming up from the alley and listening to the Oriole baseball game on his portable radio.

My Intuition

One Friday evening when everything seemed the same, we all went to Mom and Dad's to have our weekly get together. The first time I walked in front of Dad, I didn't feel anything strange happen to me, but when I walked by Dad again, a strange feeling came over me. I felt that I should grab him, hug him, and kiss him, that I was never going to see him again. I thought to myself "Stop this foolishness; there's nothing wrong. Stop imagining things." So I just took the children and went home.

The next morning the phone rang, and Mom was frantic on the phone. She asked me to come over to the house as soon as possible because something was wrong with Dad. The children and I rushed to the house to see if we could help. Mom didn't know what to do. She didn't want to call for help. She was afraid that if Dad went to the hospital, he wouldn't come home. She was also a very superstitious person. We finally persuaded her to let us call an ambulance and get him to the hospital as soon as possible. Mom was a nervous wreck. Soon after we arrived at the hospital, the doctors told us that Dad had a stroke. We did not know anything about strokes or the effects that it could have on Dad.

Dad's Stroke

If I had only followed my first intuition that something was wrong with Dad the night before, I might have been able to save him. Why, oh why, didn't I do something sooner? Now, I know the first two hours after a stroke are crucial. Why didn't I know this before? Oh how awful this was. I just believed that Mom and Dad would live forever. Dad was still young. He had just turned 65 and retired from Bethlehem Steel in August of 1972. He still had a lot of living to do. How could this happen to such a strong individual? My dad looked so strong. I was not aware of the complications of clogged arteries. Everyone thought that Dad was just fine, for he looked fantastic.

Looking back, I can remember that Dad had terrible eating habits. He would tell me that fat was good for you, and he would eat all of the fat around the pork chops and steak. He would even eat pig's feet.

I would say, "Dad how can you eat that stuff? It's gross!"

He would say, "It's good for you."

I can also remember one time Mom told me that they came home from shopping; he went over to the thermostat to turn it on, and he fell down and passed out. This was the first sign that there was something wrong with him, but when Mom wanted to take him to the doctor's he refused to go.

Of course, Mom never told any of us what happened to Dad until he had his stroke. He said that he was all right, he was so macho, and he acted as if he was strong like a bull. Dad also was a heavy smoker, and I am sure that his smoking also played a serious role in causing his stroke. He didn't smoke filtered cigarettes; he smoked the ones that gave you the full strength of the cigarettes.

On Saturday, I didn't go to work. Instead, I went to the hospital to be with Dad and Mom. The stroke had left him unable to speak, but when he saw me come into the room, he actually said, "What are you doing here?" in a slurred voice. He knew that I was supposed to be at work, even though he was so very sick. He was worried about me even then, as sick as he was. I was always his little girl.

The doctors would come and ask us what they should do, or what did we want them to do. How were we supposed to know? We weren't doctors. The first doctor who was taking care of dad went on vacation, and we were left with only interns. The summer is the worst time to ever get sick, because all the doctors go on vacation. That is why the interns kept coming over to us and asking us what we wanted them to do. We didn't have a clue. All we knew was that Dad had low blood pressure. The doctors asked us if we wanted them to give him a blood thinner, and because he had low blood pressure, we told the doctors no, when all along we were wrong. If we had said yes, it might have helped the blood clot to dissolve. But my question to the doctors is why did they ask us and not just go ahead and give him what they knew would help him?

Every morning, I would get up early, and Mom and I would go to Mass and then we would go to the hospital, to be with Dad. There was a popular song at that time. It was called "There's Got to Be a Morning After," sung by Maureen McGovern. I would play this song every day, hoping and praying that something good would happen to Dad. Every day family members went to the hospital to visit Dad. All of his brothers and sisters loved him, and they didn't want anything bad to happen to him because they all knew what a good person he was.

When Sunday came, it was almost like a family reunion at the hospital. All of Dad's brothers and their wives and all of his sisters and their husbands were at the hospital. Now that I look back on this day, it was as if they all came to say good-bye to him. Dad was restless all day. He kept moving around in the bed as if he could not get comfortable. After all of his siblings left, it was our time to say good night to Dad. We all left except for Johnny, who stayed in the hospital with him on Sunday night. Vincent and Johnny took turns every night to stay with Dad so he would not be left alone in the hospital. After I said goodnight to Dad, I thought that I should have said, "Hurry up and come home Dad, because I need something fixed at the house," but I didn't want to stress him out any more than he already was. I left without telling him how very much I needed him. We thought he would be safe with Johnny there with him.

The Phone Call

Early the next morning, I got a phone call from Aunt Lena. She woke me up and told me that we had to go get Mom and go to the hospital immediately. I was a mess, still living in a fantasy world and still believing that Dad would be all right. Mom didn't have a phone in her bedroom upstairs, and she could not hear the phone ringing downstairs. We had to go to the house and wake Mom up, and then we all went to the hospital. We drove to the hospital in silence, praying for Dad.

When we got there we found out the horrible truth, Dad had died on August 13, 1973. By the time Mom and I got there, Dad's body was already cold. We were too late. We never got the chance to say good-bye to him. The nurses wanted to give me a tranquilizer, because I was crying hysterically, but I refused it. It was positively horrible. Everyone was crying. We told the nurses and doctors that something was wrong with him Sunday night, but they didn't do a thing to find out why he was so uncomfortable. All along it was the blood clot from the stroke that was traveling in his body, and it had traveled to his heart and killed him. His life was over.

Johnny told us later that he slept on the wrong side of Dad, and that Dad had gotten out of bed and fallen down. By the time the doctors and nurses came to work on him, there was nothing that they could do for him even though they tried, they worked on Dad for a long time. They pushed Johnny out of the room, and all of the phone numbers were left in the room. This is why Johnny had to call Aunt Lena and Uncle Mimi to bring all of us to the hospital.

Everyone was so distraught; what would we do now without Dad? What would we do? I cried for days. I couldn't eat a thing. I had lost the most important person in my life the only one that truly cared for me. What would I do without Dad? Who would take care of me like he did? Who would love me like he did? My heart was aching.

Carmen's Funeral

The funeral for Dad was held at Zannino's Funeral Home at Conkling and Gough Streets. Two viewing rooms were needed to accommodate all the relatives, neighbors, and friends who came to pay their respects. Mr. and Mrs. Zannino knew how sad the family was, so they took good care of us. Many of Uncle Mimi's friends sent care packages of food. We received a huge platter of crab cakes from Mr. Bud's Restaurant, and Mr. Vacarro made desserts for us. All the local politicians came by, including Mayor Schaefer, Senator Bonvenia, Senator Mikulski, Congresswoman Bentley, former Mayor D'Alesandro, and Governor Mandel. After the funeral mass at Our Lady of Pompei, Uncle Mimi arranged for a police escort to guide a procession of more than two hundred cars. It seemed to me that all of Highlandtown mourned the loss of my father.

After Dad died, our family went adrift. We had all believed that he was so strong. How could a person of such great strength die? It was the first time we had faced our own mortality. If he could die, eventually we were all going to die. What were we going to do without him? Dad was our everything.

Aunt Lena came to me and told me that I had to move back home to help fill Mom's life up again. She said that if I went there with the children, it would help to keep her busy and take her mind off of Dad. I packed up all of my things and I gave away a lot of my furniture and household things, and I moved with the children back to Mom's. Of course, the move was only two blocks away.

Although I tried to help fill up Mom's life with the children, nothing seemed to work. Mom missed her true love tremendously. No matter what I tried to do to help her, nothing seemed to work. She was lost without Dad. She had lost the love of her life, and she didn't know what to do without him because he was her everything. Johnny told us that when he would come home on occasion, that the two of them would be lying on the couch together arm in arm. They still were very much in love with each other.

A while after this, Rosie and Bernie conceived their first child. Rosie had been trying for a long time to get pregnant. When we would meet on Fridays at Mom and Dad's for our gathering, this was the topic that consumed our whole conversation. I told Rosie that she was trying too hard, and that she had to relax more. After Dad died, and their mind was on something else, they were able to conceive. Actually, the whole time Dad was in the hospital, they were sleeping in Mom and Dad's bed to be close to the family if needed. We suspect that conception took place in that bed, which led us all to believe the same thing: Dad was coming back to us.

The Returning

Mom was getting excited about the birth of Rosie's baby. I know that when she was by herself, Dad consumed her thoughts, for after all they had been together since before 1937. She did everything for him, and now that he was gone she was lost. She didn't know what to do without him. Now that Rosie was pregnant, it provided her with something to take her mind off of Dad.

Mom threw her whole time into planning Rosie's shower. Mom and I made all of the preparations for the shower. I told her that it would be better to have cold sandwiches, potato salad, and dessert, rather than her traditional spaghetti and meatballs, and she agreed with me. I prepared all of the lunchmeat trays, and they turned out beautiful. We put aside one night to make all of the favors for the shower. Mom had invited all of our aunts and cousins to the shower, and she even got Uncle Mimi to let her have the Democratic Club hall for this special evening. Mom did everything for her family and her extended family, and everyone wanted to repay her for all of the kindness that she had bestowed upon them. All our relatives attended the shower, and it was another great time had by all.

As it got closer to Rosie's due date, the excitement kept building. Mom couldn't wait to see the new baby. Finally, one morning, Mom came to me as I was sleeping, and she said, "Leonora, Rosie, and Bernie went to the hospital. She is ready to have the baby." I knew that Mom wanted to be there with her own baby, so I got up and took her to the hospital.

On Monday, April 29, 1974, at four o'clock in the afternoon, Brian was born. We all knew that Dad had come back to us.

The love that Mom and Dad shared is hard to find today. Their love for each other was unmatched. Every time they looked into each other's eyes they had an everlasting look of love. They acted like they never wanted any kiss to be their last kiss. They wanted to be together forever.

I will search for this kind of love all of my days until I find my own true love.

Afterword

After leaving my husband, I had to get a second job to adequately provide for my children, so I missed a lot of time with them. I tried to make up for lost time by keeping them with me on my two days off. I took them ice skating in the winter and swimming during the summer. We went to the movies or just watched TV together at home, and that was enough to make all of us happy. We enjoyed many vacations together. The three of us had a great time being with one another. We didn't need anything fancy, just each other.

I managed to send both girls to high school, but I could not afford to send them to college. What a shame because they were both very smart. Michelle and Anna both became managers at different Wendy's fast food restaurants, they met their husbands, and went on to have children of their own. Now Anna has three children and Michelle, who recently lost her husband (the love of her life, as well), has two children.

My mother, Phyllis DiPietro, passed away on June 27, 1986.

Just like Mom and Dad taught us while growing up, we—the family—remain very close today.

When you are in Baltimore, visit Little Italy and stop in Sabatino's to say "hi." I'm still waiting on tables, beating the odds, and having a peachy life.

Acknowledgments

I wish to thank the following friends and supporters who believed in my story and my ability to tell it:

Michael and Suzy Olesker, who were the first people to tell me I had a heartwarming story; Sharon Miller, who spent many long hours editing my manuscript several times; Father Bob Albright, who checked the spelling and told me the story was good; Father Lou Trotta, who loved the story and introduced me to the man who enhanced the cover from a small black and white photo, Bob Gussio; Christine McPhail, who gave me the encouragement to go on with the writing and who told me "You have a movie here!"; Barry Levinson, who told me to write scenes more dramatically because Hollywood wants drama; Gregg Wilhelm, who took enough interest in my story to publish the book; and Robyn Barberry, who told me how much she loved the story and edited the final version.

Last but not least, thank you Susan Boyle. In the spring of 2009, just as I was feeling down in the dumps about finishing this memoir and whether it would ever be published, Ms. Boyle was gaining international attention. Even though she sang amazingly, there was such flap over her plain appearance, but it occurred to me that sometimes important gifts come wrapped in plain paper—like my story. Ms. Boyle had the courage to go on stage and blow people away with her beautiful voice.

So I said to myself, "If she has the courage to do it, so can I."

CITYLIT
PRESS

CityLit Press's mission is to provide a venue for writers who might otherwise be overlooked by larger publishers due to the literary quality or regional focus of their projects. It is the imprint of nonprofit CityLit Project, founded in Baltimore in 2004.

CityLit nurtures the culture of literature in Baltimore and throughout Maryland by creating enthusiasm for literature, building a community of avid readers and writers, and opening opportunities for young people and diverse audiences to embrace the literary arts.

Thank you to our major supporters: the Maryland State Arts Council, the Baltimore Office of Promotion and The Arts, and the Baltimore Community Foundation. More information and documentation is available at www.guidestar.org.

Additional support is provided by individual contributors. Financial support is vital for sustaining the on-going work of the organization. Secure, on-line donations can by made at our web site, click on "Donate."

CityLit is a member of the Greater Baltimore Cultural Alliance, the Maryland Association of Nonprofit Organizations, and the Writers' Conferences and Centers division of the Association of Writers and Writing Programs (AWP).

Baltimore magazine named the press's first book a "Best of Baltimore" and commented: "CityLit Project has blossomed into a local treasure on a variety of fronts—especially its public programming and workshops—and it recently added a publishing imprint to its list of minor miracles."

For submission guidelines, information about CityLit Press's two poetry chapbook contests, and all the programs and services offered by CityLit, please visit www.citylitproject.org.

Nurturing the culture of literature.

CPSIA information can be obtained at www.ICGtesting.com
Printed in the USA
267692BV00004B/28/P